# DATE DUE

| | | |
|---|---|---|
| | | |
| OCT 6 01 | | |
| NO 1 5 07 | | |
| | | |
| | | |
| | | |
| | | |
| | | |
| | | |
| | | |
| | | |
| | | |
| | | |
| | | |
| | | |
| | | |
| | | |
| | | |

DEMCO 38-296

# TEAMS
# AND
# TECHNIQUES
## FOR WORLD CLASS IMPROVEMENT

PUBLISHED IN THE UNITED STATES OF AMERICA
THOMAS R. KING
343 CRESTVIEW DRIVE
FRANKLIN, PENNSYLVANIA 16323
PHONE (814) 432-5943

ISBN 0-9652622-0-0

# CONTENTS

## INTRODUCTION

## TEAMS AND TECHNIQUES FOR WORLD CLASS IMPROVEMENT

# INTRODUCTION

## TEAMS OF THE ANIMAL KINGDOM

There is no shortage of words or terms to describe an arrangement where two or more people come together for a purpose: TEAM is one of them.

Each term brings with it some baggage and the power to stir one's emotions. Posses, mobs, cliques, and gangs are generally suspect. On a lesser scale, so are committees – as evidenced by the oft quoted clichés, such as:

- For God so loved the world He did not send a committee
- A camel is a horse designed by a committee.

Teams, however, except for the Chicago Cubs, who have not won a major event in nearly a century, have a favorable connotation. Teams imply teamwork and a sense of collective spirit – subordinating personal prominence to the benefit of the whole.

My earliest thoughts about teaming came from barnyard animals. Living on a farm, insulated from many of the worldly distractions of the day, I became a keen observer of happenings in that arena.

Teams of horses fascinated me; particularly at the annual Jacktown Fair where large Belgian and Morgan horses strutted their stuff. Several teams of horses were pitted against each other in a weight pulling contest.

The object of the contest was for an owner to hook up his team of horses to designated weights in the dirt roadway. Then, at a signal from the judge, the team would attempt to pull the weight down the roadway – urged and guided by the owner or handler, walking alongside. This action was spirited: commensurate with whistles, shouting, and flying dust. Distance pulled was measured within a specific time frame. This sequence was subsequently repeated, adding additional weights, until one team eventually triumphed and was declared the winner.

Observing this activity, one soon learned that victory was not always to the biggest or strongest horses; but, rather to the congruency and harmony with which the team pulled and moved together. Often the horses were out of sync with each other – one pulling alone, then stopped, staggered by the load; while the other, late in starting, struggled in turn. This spelled failure. Today these pulling contests are largely replaced by tractor pulls – the romance is gone and the victor determined by whomever has the

1

fattest wallet, and procures the most horsepower.

This phenomenon of teaming was also evident back on the family farm where my father used horses in plowing and cultivating between corn rows. The tandem horse team had to be in harmony or the corn rows would be wiped out; and sometimes were much to dad's dismay. Another observation was that it was not the horse team alone – but, my father who complemented this systematic team. He was, in fact, the developer, trainer, and team builder of this fine team and the on-going master or coach. You might wonder what the outcome of incidentally borrowing a horse from a neighbor and matching up with one of yours for the afternoon's work would be. I can tell you. Chances are slim to none that success would be swift. It would require practice, and some compatibility between the horses. It would require some structuring as to which horse performed better on the right or left traces. Individual strength and endurance attributes would be determining factors also.

Similarly, anyone can see the logic of a sports director not venturing into the street to grab the first five people he or she met to form a basketball team; or a singing quintet. Then, consider this: why would it make any sense to appoint random individuals from an organization to a team where their main virtues were availability and body temperature, and expect them to perform successfully?

Yet, collectively, it is precisely what often happens in industrial, business and service sector settings.

## SHEEP MARCH AND THE IMMACULATE TEAM

During a recent summer, my wife and I visited Price, Utah on a business trip. Having a little extra time, we returned to Salt Lake City Airport via the scenic route – past Hiawatha, population 249, and up through Huntington Canyon.

To say the scenery was exhilarating, particularly to an easterner, would be to say too little. But, notwithstanding the grandeur of those mighty peaks of the Wasatch Mountain Range, we came across one of the most spectacular sights or events, that I will ever see. On a crisp, snow-capped, sun-splashed morning, there they were: swarms of sheep being systematically moved miles down Highway 31 to a new grazing location. There seemed to be a million of them. Although a farm boy at birth, I had never realized the totally team nature required to relocate a sheep herd down a public highway to new pastures.

Advised later, there were 2,400 sheep in the herd, separated into two groups a mere few yards apart. At any time, if individual sheep were to act alone, they could have scattered into as many directions as there were sheep. A poorly organized team effort would have allowed it. Yet, the procession was flawless.

It was commanded by a combined team of animals and people, each doing a specific job. Parked on the side of the road, it was easy to observe by the trained eye what each team member's role was, and how they were doing it.

A large, white, gentle-looking dog, probably a Samoyed, led the pack. Her job was to walk ever so slowly without exciting the masses, essentially leading the pack as a drum major might. Then, there were what I would call the rounders: Border Collies whose attitude was quite different than "Whitey," the leader. They were all movement, spirit, and agitation, rounding up strays and nipping at the backs of legs. The nipping occurred to all those in the back row as a reminder to keep bunched and in line. Five riders, on high horseback, skirted the perimeter, did some whistling, and were probably there to open gates and perhaps pick up the lame, if any. Last, in the procession, were a truck and utility vehicle to protect the rear from fast approaching vehicles.

To say I have been involved in over a ton of committees, teams, or task forces during my career is an understatement. Never have I seen a team so perfectly designed with specific roles and perfect execution to do a job as this one.

We can learn a lot from the sheep team.

---

## WHERE TWO OR MORE ARE GATHERED

| | | |
|---|---|---|
| 40 MULE TEAM | CHOIR | CONVENTION |
| POSSE | DIVISION | JURY |
| MOB | BAND | PRIDE |
| TROUPE | TASK FORCE | REGIMENT |
| CAST | GANG | BATTALION |
| PAIR | CLIQUE | THRONG |
| ASSEMBLY | TEAM | GROUP |
| OCTET | CREW | QUARTET |
| FAMILY | BEVY | COUNCIL |
| TRIO | HERD | COMMITTEE |
| PLATOON | LITTER | PANEL |
| DYAD | POD | SEXTET |

AND A FEW MORE

---

## RABBIT HUNTING TEAM

Some of my early appreciation of team dynamics came as a result of hunting rabbits. The homestead I lived on as a fifteen year old was ideal for a budding nimrod.

Civilization lay only to the East, fronting the Monongahela River – incidentally, the Monongahela being one of the few major rivers in the northern hemisphere to flow North. Woodlands bordered the farm in all other directions (thousands of acres).

Above all, to hunt rabbits effectively, one needed a talented beagle. A customer on my newspaper route provided us two pups from his dog's litter. One was a somewhat unusually colored black and tan male – we called Peg, the other a female named Meg. So, Peg, Meg, and I became a pretty decent team with complimenting skills.

Meg, as it turns out, had no nose trailing scent to speak of, but was remarkable at rooting hares out of brush piles. Peg provided the complementary skills needed. Conversely, he liked the paths, avoiding the brush, but was terrific in staying on a rabbit's tail at just the right place to bring them full circle past yours truly.

Although the rabbit team venue might seem remote from an industrial world application, it really has many of the same ingredients needed for team success, such as: a

3

defined objective, team players, team dynamics, training, skills, resources, and application. And, something else – Enthusiasm.

One of my fondest memories in my growing years was opening the dog pen and watching the dogs enthusiastically prepare for the hunt.

## TRANSITION TO THE PRESENT

The past seems so near and yet so far. It's a long way from the calmness of my boyhood farm days to the frenetic pace exacted by a global marketplace. A marketplace where the basis of competition assures that organizations will become proficient in the use of resource teams, innovative techniques, and strategies. For not to do so will assure that they will cease to be prominent players. This work highlights experiences gathered in a work career spanning four major corporations and an equal number of decades. Nothing remains the same except for memories.

# TEAMS
# AND
# TECHNIQUES
## FOR WORLD CLASS IMPROVEMENT

# CHAPTER ONE

## NATURE OF TEAMS

### TEAM DEFINITION

A team can be thought of as a small collection of people who join together to address a particular assignment.

Unless, of course, you are talking about a team as described by the American Heritage Dictionary: "two or more draft animals used to pull a vehicle or farm implement".

Muscle, obedience, experience, and stamina is required for one team; people skills for the other.

In the case of ordinary business teams, the issue relates to a group of people working together to pursue a defined objective. The team will have a life together, interacting over the course of the project, and then disband. Team members, at least in part, will probably have worked with each other on a previous assignment.

> *Great discoveries and achievements invariably involve the cooperation of many minds*
>
> *– Alexander Graham Bell*

### SYSTEMS VS. TEAMS

Many of my relatives were farmers.

My Uncle Jim's daily routine involved milking cows, accumulating the milk in five gallon stainless steel cans, and storing in the roadside milk house. A trucker would pick up the milk, leaving empty cans for subsequent trips. From there, the milk traveled to a middle man processor, on to a retailer, and eventually to a customer.

Is this a team? No, it is a collection of people, each doing a function independent of each other. And, in truth, many of the people would not recognize each other through a chance meeting on the street. What you have here is a system rather than a team.

# TEAMS AS COMPARED TO COMMITTEES

Terms are many and varied for describing groups that are formed to work on specific tasks.

Although having similarities, chief among them being a group effort and a task in mind, there is a distinction between teams and other collective forms.

A team is usually thought of as being more amenable to subordinating personal prominence as individuals than perhaps a task force or committee. Another nuance of a team that differs, if only by degree, is the spirit of togetherness. The spirit of a team is manifested in the theater in the likes of the three musketeers; all for one, and one for all.

A simplified comparison of nominal differences between a team and a committee are expressed in the chart.

---

## WHAT TEAMS AND COMMITTEES DO:
## A SIMPLIFIED VIEW

| COMMITTEES | TEAMS |
|---|---|
| Decide what charities to support | Reduce throughput time |
| Facilitate company picnics | Make paradigm shifts |
| Blue ribbon fact finding | Enhance customer value |
| Administer funeral flower fund | Handle big assignments |
| Hear grievances and mitigate | Cause change |
| Likely to be large | Typically 5-7 members |
| Regional representation | Specialized skills |
| Spend money | Enhance value |
| Majority vote | Consensus by merit |
| Review recommendations | Develop and implement |

---

## Characteristics of a Team

- Group has a project or task that begs an outcome.

- Group will have some significant clock time together.

- Team is often appointed by and held accountable to a higher body.

- Members are ordinarily selected because of possessing particular expertise, skills set, or knowledge in a needed area.

- Members tend to be appointed rather than solicited via a volunteering process.

- Teams organized for a specific purpose have a life, and an ending.

- Teams are organized because they are superior to an individual effort for the task at hand.

- Team will function as an informal group having face-to-face relationships.

| CATEGORICAL TYPES OF TEAMS | | | |
|---|---|---|---|
| Public Safety | Medical | Task | Hospice |
| Sports | Research | News | Social |
| Search | Attack | Judicial | Business |
| Beasts of Burden | Rescue | Policital | Canvassing |

Teams flourish in everyday life. The reason they exist is that jobs are too big, too complex, or need to be done quicker than one person alone can do it. A team is a gathering of knowledge, skills, and multiple hands.

Within each category of teams can be many related sub types. For instance, under public safety, you could have a raft of focused teams such as:

- Hazardous Waste Team
- Chemical Spill Team
- Water Safety Team
- Robbery Squad Team

- Fire Fighting Team
- Fire Prevention Team
- Domestic Violence Team
- Bunko Squad Team

Illustrated: Public Safety Teams Category

# TEAM CHARTERS AND MISSIONS

Clarity of the team's objective upfront in the process is a big plus. Sometimes, and perhaps most of the time, the objective is clear enough.

A rescue team attempting to recover a small child trapped in a pipe probably knows exactly what the objective is. A safe recovery with the least trauma at the earliest possible moment. In less obvious business situations, the objective is often fuzzier. And, the less a team knows where it is going, it will take longer and create a lot of wasted energy along the way.

That is why team sponsors have placed a lot of importance on framing the object in a suitable way. The objective often takes on more powerful connotations with such definers as charter, mission statement, and vision. It is not rare that a team will spend an inordinate amount of time dealing with vision and mission statements. The end result is often platitudes of dogma which is seldom understood or remembered later during team dynamics.

I do not think it a terrible injustice to suggest that if all vision and mission statements were laying end to end, all that could be said is that they were laying end to end. One definition of the teams charter that makes sense, follows as illustrated.

> *Team charter is a formal document stating the team's mission along with the principles, resources, and guidelines under which it will operate.*

Nevertheless, the intention and the need is clear. In hierarchical structures the staff members possessing of power must act as a team in planning and executing strategy. To vector energies in the same direction the various functional managers must act as one; and exhibit the same interdependent and support characteristics as any focused team. Mutual trust is a key ingredient of the relationships and must be earned by deeds rather than intentions.

Hierarchical teams, as a rule, are seldom organized collectively as a focused task team; that is a team that is organized to handle a particular project, and then disband once it is completed. Rather they are thought of as a permanent team, merely by being closely knit in the common hierarchy. The same goes for a subteam within the functional hierarchy.

## TYPES OF TEAMS IN ORGANIZATION

There exists, a myriad of team types that have found application in business, non-profit, and volunteer organizations. The discussion here will focus on four broad categories, being:

- Hierarchical Teams
- Continuous Purpose Teams
- High Performance Teams
- Virtual Teams

## Hierarchical Teams

A hierarchical team as viewed consists of a functional manager and her reporting staff. In a large business organization, it is likely that this body will be thought of as the executive core rather than a team; albeit, that the group is expected to operate as a team in harmony with each other. As you drop down levels in the organizations, more subteams develop.

Certainly, at the top of the organizational apex, one would expect that the staff would perform as a well-oiled team. It is obvious, however, that that is not universally the case. Obvious because of the litany of articles and abounding clichés that describe the interaction of organizational functions as stovepipes or "walled-in departments". Turf issues are big.

# HIERARCHICAL TEAMS

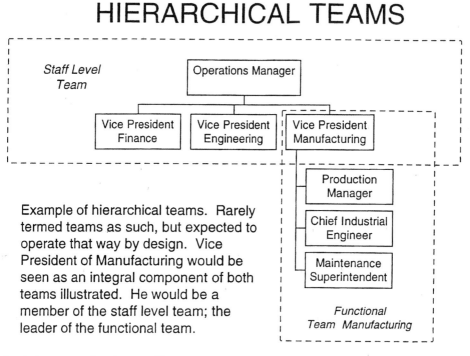

Example of hierarchical teams. Rarely termed teams as such, but expected to operate that way by design. Vice President of Manufacturing would be seen as an integral component of both teams illustrated. He would be a member of the staff level team; the leader of the functional team.

## Continuous Purpose Teams

Continuous purpose teams have some similarity to a focused team in that they draw talented team members from multi-functional disciplines. Also, they are formed for a particular purpose; but are usually broader in scope than a focused project team.

Continuous purpose teams differ from other teams in their staying power. They have a continuous life. Examples would be idea review teams in a continuous improvement program or suggestion evaluation teams. These teams would have an extended life with no end in sight as long as the particular program flourished. Team membership would also be different in that it is likely, and advantageous, to rotate team members over time. It is also good practice to stagger the rotation of team members serving on the team rather than make wholesale changes at the same time.

## Focused Project Teams

Focused project teams are quickly identifiable as being different from hierarchical teams. For openers, they are called a team and were organized to focus on a particular project. Once that project is complete, in all likelihood, their team will dissolve.

Focused teams usually draw on the needed knowledge and skills sets for the project by searching the matrix organization for team members from a variety of functions.

In the main, the appointed team members from the multi-functional areas participate part time on the team project while continuing to do their chief responsibilities. Administratively, they will continue to report to their immediate supervisor.

This is not always the case depending on the importance and priority of the team project, and who is championing the effort. Some of the larger heralded projects such as factory of the future or reengineering efforts require full time autonomous assignments.

As a team, a focused project team is much more formal than a hierarchical team. Meetings are planned and conducted with minutes and action plans being an integral part of the process.

## High Performance Teams

High performance teams are achievers. They are fluid, well modulated, temperate, and purposeful. They are winners.

High performance teams are not assembled overnight. I suppose it could happen; if so, it would be a rarity. Rather, high performance teams are normally an evolution – beginning first with symbiotic pairs and progressing over time. Historically, organization management is usually in the form of a pyramid. It doesn't make much difference whether you are talking about a business, volunteer organization, armed forces, or religious faith, a pyramid is the rule.

To effect major change, one must collaborate with fellow employees who report to different masters. Through experience, one finds those people in various functions who are willing and able to lend a hand. Beginning with this favorable rapport, the continuing mutual contact eventually involves team efforts with others of a similar mind and capability. The team progresses from being an informal virtual team to a visible high performance team.

## Virtual/High Performance Teams

Much interest is being expressed about the building of high performance teams who become the heart of a company's survival strategy. It is correctly anticipated that teams will replace much of the vertically integrated hierarchies that exist today. My feeling is that, in all likelihood, it will occur more often and completely in smaller organizations than larger ones due to the sheer nature of size.

In large organizations, there will be more involvement by teams in the day to day

# CHAPTER TWO
## TEAMWORK: THE ART OF WORKING TOGETHER

> *No one can whistle a symphony. It takes an orchestra to play it.*
> — H.E. Luccock

Everyone can understand and appreciate the cooperative teamwork that is needed in symphonies and teams in the sports world.

You may or may not have noticed the intense degree of camaraderie and teamwork among firefighters. They work in a dangerous occupation where their full attention is given to public safety. Many fire departments are made up of non-paid volunteers who willingly form the cluster who handles local emergencies ranging from traffic control to drownings to automobile accidents to hazardous waste spills, and, of course, fire prevention and firefighting. Often, they are faced with a life or death situation and, when a sad event occurs with a fellow member, all join in formal tribute and eulogy to the fallen. Teamwork is an essential ingredient in the process. The relationships are so tight that the unit is often termed a "Brotherhood." The feeling is there to match the statement.

What is not exposed, as well to the general public is the critical application of teamwork needed in less formal teams in business and volunteer organizations.

---

### TEAMWORK DEFINITIONS

*Work done by several associates with each doing a part but all subordinating personal prominence to the efficiency of the whole*

*Teamwork is the ability to work together toward a common vision. The ability to direct individual accomplishment toward organizational objectives*

*Simply stated, it is less me and more we.*

---

The essence of teamwork can be preached until it sounds like dogma or a platitude designed to suppress individual egos. Preaching alone doesn't get it. It must be developed in a team, over time, by intentions and actions which result in mutual trust, respect, and a driving will to accomplish the task. Teamwork implies the use of team members skills and knowledge, collectively, while committed to common causes.

One interesting aspect of teamwork surfaced in the now defunct Pittsburgh Spirit Soccer team. Stan Terlicki was, to the noticeability of all the team, the best individual performer. A scoring star, he was the only Spirit team member named to the league's All-Star Game. Additionally, he was the team's highest paid player. Nevertheless, Terlicki was benched for a considerable time due to what management expressed as a "lack of team play." Spirit General Manager, Chris Wright, in a newspaper article, said, "We either have to trade him (Terlicki) or bring in new players who can play with Stan." Incidentally, the team's win-loss record fared no better without Stan in the lineup, than when he played.

## Clarity of Purpose

Some teams flounder because there has been no clearly defined objective early in the process. Teams experiencing this seem unable to separate abstraction from concreteness, and mistake activity for accomplishment.

It would seem moot to say that clarity of objective should be a paramount upfront issue in the formation of a team. Why then is the team objective frequently unclear?

One reason is that many teams are organized as a somewhat exploratory exercise. For example, two trendy initiatives of the early nineties, Reengineering and Total Quality Management (TQM), spanned numerous committees and teams that collapsed under their own weight. Occasionally the appetite was too big, the hype too superficial, and the direction too muddy.

Clarity of purpose alone does not necessarily get the job done in an effective manner. At the onset, the project is somewhat analogous to planning a trip: you know where you want to go, but there is an array of choices for getting there – some better than others. Obviously, if one travels north when the destination is south, little progress will be made until the direction changes.

So it is with team members. Each individual will have ideas on how best to proceed with a project, and they will differ from each other. The problem occurs when they differ significantly and are not vectored in similar focus. Mathematically, we can easily calculate what happens when forces are marshaled in similar direction and what occurs when they oppose. The same effect happens with teams although not as quantitatively apparent.

## Multi-Function Team Structure

It is difficult to imagine a complex project or problem that does not require multi-function input to solve effectively. To a great extent, a typical organization is structured as a hierarchy leading upward to an apex and sprinkled throughout with individual departments and functions. This structure, along with fragile egos and often physical barriers or walls between departments, limits effective communications and joint ventures. Some aptly termed the condition as functional stovepipes.

To counteract this dilemma, teams are formed with individuals from various functions gathered as a team to cooperatively deal with an assigned project. Decisions on which functions should be represented on a team is a judgment call depending on the project nature. For example, a product hardware project team might consist of a project engineer, methods engineer, buyer, production worker, and an accountant. Whereas, a paperwork project might include a clerk, secretary, value engineer, a buyer, and a systems person.

## FUNCTIONAL STOVEPIPES

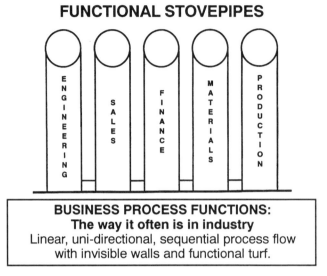

**BUSINESS PROCESS FUNCTIONS:**
**The way it often is in industry**
Linear, uni-directional, sequential process flow
with invisible walls and functional turf.

## Idea Review Teams: Size & Shape

The number of teams, team size, and team shape is entirely dependent upon the business and the number of ideas being processed in a given year. For a major manufacturing business, having in excess of a thousand participating employees, the number of teams, and functional representation could well fit the illustration which follows. A smaller business, perhaps a service organization, might require just one idea review team such as illustrated.

In either situation, big or small organization, the teams could meet at a regularly scheduled time every second week or so. Meeting duration should be a maximum of 1-2 hour duration. During holiday or heavy vacation periods the slated times can be adjusted to suit the situation.

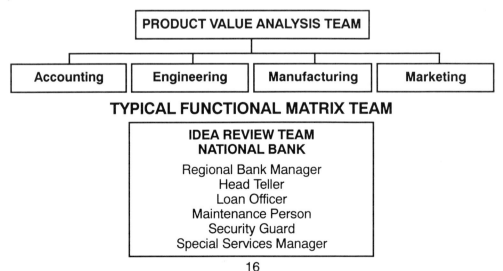

### PRODUCT VALUE ANALYSIS TEAM

| Accounting | Engineering | Manufacturing | Marketing |

**TYPICAL FUNCTIONAL MATRIX TEAM**

**IDEA REVIEW TEAM**
**NATIONAL BANK**

Regional Bank Manager
Head Teller
Loan Officer
Maintenance Person
Security Guard
Special Services Manager

## Rotation of Team Members

One final point on team member structure: while the functional representation on a team may continue permanently for the team's life, rotation of members is a good idea. Rotation allows more people to be trained in the team building process and also provides a pool of substitutes, if needed on a short term basis.

Rather than rotate all members of the team simultaneously, it is better to discharge and add new members as a percentage of team members. For example, a team of six might turn over two members each year; thus, members would be serving a staggered three year term.

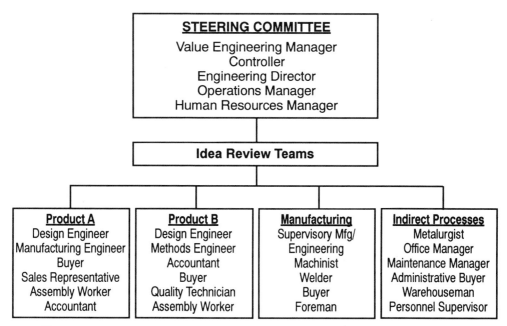

**Typical Functional Make-Up Industrial Idea Review Teams in Larger Companies**

## SPONTANEOUS TEAMS: CAN THEY WORK?

I believe it is possible on some rare occasions to spontaneously come together as a team, work through an objective during a small span of time, and then disband.

One experience I will long cherish was a visit to a sister company facility in Birmingham. My boss, who was later to become board chairman, dispatched me on a visit there with no apparent mission in mind. He just smiled mischievously and said, "Go down, you might learn something."

Arriving there, the general manager, too, was at a loss as to what my objective was, and understandably somewhat suspect at this northern invasion. At his early morning staff meeting, a severe production problem was being addressed. They were short a tubular body to complete a hydraulic cylinder used on a mobile drilling rig. No cylinder:

no shipment. Simple as that. And, the promise date to the customer was nearly sacrosanct.

Problem was this. The Louisiana subcontractor could not provide the pre-bored cylinder to the production floor in time for the finish honing operation. Subsequent assembly and shipment to customer was in great jeopardy. Turning to me, they looked askance, "Any ideas?"

Prior to becoming an engineer, I had an early career as a toolmaker and designer; a good combination for a problem such as this. I quickly sketched a bulldozer mandrel that hopefully could be powered through the tubing, opening up the cylinder in lieu of a boring operation. But, I did not think time was on our side.

However, a foreman took the sketch and ran with it, doggedly working around the clock to complete the mandrel for the morning try.

It worked! And, I was as remarkably surprised as they were. It was truly a team effort.

To my southern hosts, I immediately became a respected bona-fide member of their team, working on things for the remainder of my visit.

Our early success on the first problem was the catalyst for bringing out other projects that had been on the back burner. It was a fun time.

This story reinforces the notion that great satisfaction can come from a team or group working in harmony. Nothing breeds satisfaction like success on a difficult challenge.

# CHAPTER THREE
## TEAM PROBLEM SOLVING

### INDIVIDUAL VERSUS TEAM PROBLEM SOLVING

At least two studies in major universities have indicated that an individual working alone is a more productive thinker than a group when it comes to problem solving. I'm thinking that this outcome must have been unique to a particular situation and not usually the case.

While an individual might do better, technically speaking, in some circumstances, having a good solution to a problem is far different than having it accepted. Consequently, the acceptance of a decision by the individuals involved is often as important as the quality of the decision.

Saying this another way:

A team decision of somewhat lower quality may be more practical than a technically correct one expressed by an individual, because the team decision may be implemented quicker, easier, and perhaps at all.

One large issue is acceptance by the decision maker. The decision maker is more likely to be influenced by a team decision, particularly if a subordinate or trusted individual was involved in the study.

As Vince Pfaff put it:

*"People tend to resist that which is forced upon them: people tend to support that which they help create."*

In retrospect, the two main ingredients of an effective decision are:

• Solution must be of sound quality
• Solution must be acceptable to the decision makers

### SPHERE OF KNOWLEDGE

The sphere of knowledge concept explains the value of pooling individuals as a team to maximize knowledge. The concept is highlighted through a series of intersecting circles. Each circle will have some shared common space and some private space that it and it alone occupies. The analogy being likened to individuals on a team; there will be some common knowledge shared by some or all, and some information that each alone knows. The dotted area represents knowledge common to all members. The shaded area represents that knowledge which is known to that individual alone. The remaining solid areas are common knowledge to two or more team members. The principle being that all members are important: that one piece of data or input needed to solve a problem could be unique to a certain individual.

## Sphere of Knowledge

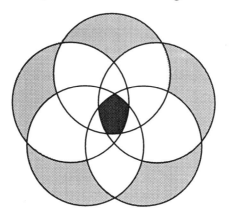

## Idea Review Team vs Individual Evaluations

Employee involvement through continuous improvement programs have been increasingly popular in small businesses as well as major corporations. Employee involvement takes on a variety of forms such as suggestion programs, work simplification efforts, problem solving groups, Quality Circles, and Value Engineering projects. Common to each of these is the quest for ideas, finding better ways to do things; improved value at lower costs, or enhanced features that increase customer satisfaction. These programs are ongoing.

Most of the ideas generated will be submitted in writing, or recorded as such during circle meetings.

The next important consideration then becomes how to evaluate and implement the ideas.

One system used to evaluate ideas is the direct approach. The administrator or continuous improvement program leader will direct the idea to a lone individual who would seem to have authority and expertise for ruling on it's merits and implementation. This process would seem most efficient to a bystander as there are no middle-men involved to clutter the matter.

But, there is a downside to the straight line being the shortest distance between two points. That is, you miss the dialogue, confirmation, and devil's advocacy that would be a positive by-product of a team review. Not all decision makers hampered by a shortage of resources or an attitude react positively to ideas causing them additional work.

Let's see how this concept works using an idea review team on a not uncommon scenario. The leader presents, to the gathered team, an idea from a shop worker:

Leader: "Let's see what we have here. Barney Mains from the assembly floor suggests adding a chamber to the X-16 pin and enlarging the bolt tolerance to permit faster assembly. As the Product Engineer, Bill, what do you think?"

Bill, the Product Engineer: "I don't think it will save enough time to warrant changing the drawing. Changes cost money. Besides, I don't know when we could get to it."

Ron, the Methods Engineer: "But Bill, Barney has a point. That pin assembly delays us about 15 minutes on every job. That's a lot of time."

Krista, the Accountant: "I don't know about your time to change the drawing Bill, but that is an item that causes a significant variance every time it hits the shop."

Leader: "Bill, what do you think? Can you work it in?"

Bill: "Okay, you have me outnumbered. I'll do it. I didn't realize it was that much of a problem."

NOTE: The chances of this particular idea being implemented had a team not been involved under the stated conditions would have been nil.

---

Advantages that a team brings to bear on idea review teams and similar efforts are:

- Diverse inputs on a subject that team members might have direct knowledge.

- Peer pressure for all members to get in the spirit of the task. Feedback and follow through.

- A sounding board to gain consensus for a decision.

- Collective wisdom might enable a team to massage an unworkable idea and modify the solution to make it practical.

- A team can focus on all open ideas in progress and receive new ideas in a forum setting; whereas, ideas distributed directly to idea evaluators from the leader might be widely scattered and difficult to manage.

---

## EFFECT OF TEAM SIZE

The number of members in a team is an important issue.

Optimum team size has been a heated topic of debate not only in the workplace, but also in after-hours social taprooms as well. It's an ongoing argument.

In the same spirit that one defends his inheritance, some practitioners advocate a precise number of bodies on a project team. Albeit that the preferences range from a low of three, to break ties I think, anywhere up to a battalion. The ideal number most often expressed is five; matching the number of fingers and toes on a limb. Many project managers advocate five as correct.

The reality is that the job is the boss. The situation will determine what is needed in a specific case. In retrospect, the quantity of members is surely less important than the collective grey matter, skills, initiative, and attitudes assembled to get the job done.

Perhaps a good rule of thumb is that the team should only be as large as necessary to do the job within the scope of parameters. With respect to putting a quantitative number on projects, my experience suggests that a team size of 5-7 permanent members will handle ninety percent of projects encountered.

As different input is needed during the project life, experts can be brought in and out of team meetings as Ad Hoc members.

Group size has a direct effect on potential productivity. All else being equal, potential productivity of teams would increase in direct proportion to members added: two members having twice the potential of one, three having three times the potential, and so on.

But, this is hardly the case. Not all members will possess the same level of intellect, expertise, skills, and experience. Nor will all functions represented have equal impact on the subject being worked. As members are added, there will be more redundancy of already accumulated knowledge and less new insight and thought.

## Process Losses

Added members, particularly in groups larger than seven, bring a certain degree of clutter and inefficiency. Even in a disciplined group, if one member talks, the others are in a listening mode. Being social, humans have a tendency to introduce personal chatter such as sports happenings, the weather, ailments, and a myriad of other time consumers. I am not advocating eliminating all soft conversation from meetings. People are people – not cattle. Some cushion time is necessary to build harmony and understanding; however, process losses occur, and, if not reasonably controlled by a disciplined group, the losses can be heavy and detract from the team's output.

## Actual Productivity

Actual productivity then is a factor affecting the quality and timing of the team's output. The measure of a team's success lies in favorable outcomes and, failing that, doing the best job possible under compelling circumstances that denied an opportunity for a wanted outcome.

## SOCIAL LOAFING PHENOMENON

Early social scientists wrestled with two perspectives on the effect of group size on team performance. One perspective, Holism, held that the whole is greater than the sum of its parts. Much of this theory had its basis in Synergetics, from the Greek word Synergos, meaning "working together." It was thought that the interaction of the various skills that team members brought to bear produced a one plus one equals three effect.

| Many hands make light the load | Too many cooks spoil the broth |

However, later studies did little to support this perspective and a new, more popular view prevailed: Reductionism. Reductionism holds that the whole group is, at best and probably not, equal to the sum of its parts.

Further, later studies supported the reductionist view and identified a detractor to the group process. This detractor was called "Social Loafing." Credit for this finding was attributed to a German psychologist named Ringelmann. One experiment he conducted was a rope pulling task: first with individuals acting alone – measuring their ability via a strain gauge. The collective sum of their individual efforts was totaled, then compared with the result found later when the team pulled together. The team's performance fell short of that obtained in total by the individual's acting alone. Later, studies in controlled settings mirrored this same result.

I witnessed the same effect during two earthy observations. A colleague at work convinced about eight of us to transfer an upright piano from a seller's house to his. Part of the convincing was that half a dozen of the team, sans myself, stopped off at the local pub for some quick libation. Later, when the actual heaving and moving of the heavy piano occurred, I think I must have shouldered three quarters of the load. Social Loafing! With a little faked grimace of the face, who could tell who was lifting and who was not?

Another quick example of Social Loafing by individuals within a group occurred as a band performed on the football playing field. Who knew that a couple of freshman clarinet players, one being my future wife, had enough trouble marching to the routines that notes seldom flew from the instrument? But, among a myriad of clarinets and bugles, it proved no telling effect.

Reasons that have been suggested for the phenomenon of Social Loafing are:

- Submaximal goal setting

- When more members are available, certain individuals may not have to work as hard

- Individuals can hide in the crowd, virtually unnoticed

- Motivation and recognition for individual performance on a team may not be equal to the individual's higher performance. Feeling shortchanged, they might reduce their output more in line with the group average.

Social loafing becomes much less of a possibility if two elements are in place during the team process:

- All team members share evenly in the accountability for the successful handling of the project. Accountability should be more than just mouthed: it should be incumbent upon all members.

- All team members will benefit from a job well done and be recognized accordingly.

# EFFECTS OF TEAM SIZE

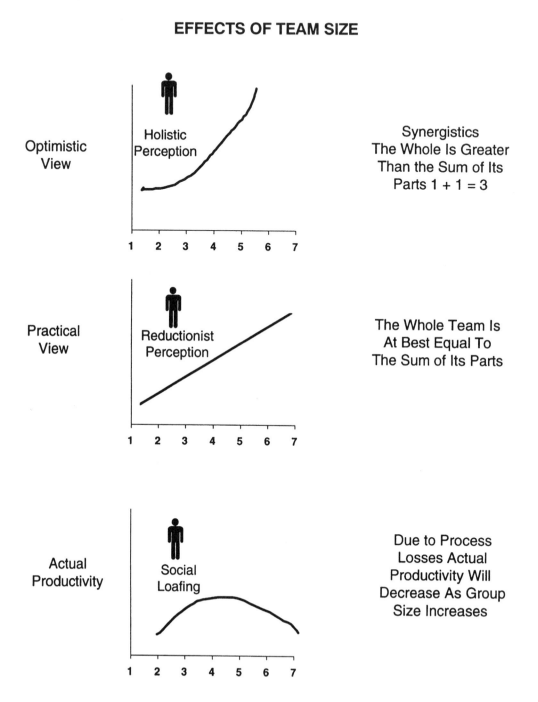

Optimistic View

Holistic Perception

Synergistics
The Whole Is Greater
Than the Sum of Its
Parts $1 + 1 = 3$

Practical View

Reductionist Perception

The Whole Team Is
At Best Equal To
The Sum of Its Parts

Actual Productivity

Social Loafing

Due to Process
Losses Actual
Productivity Will
Decrease As Group
Size Increases

# Optimum Team Size – 5 to 7 Rule

*"What is the optimum team size?"*

As stated earlier, rather than an absolute number, the recommended size would be stated as a range. That range, for ordinary manageable projects or subprojects, would normally be five to seven members: with Ad Hoc members added as necessary to supplement the group dynamics process. Call it the "5-7 Rule".

However, nothing is sacrosanct about the size. Size is determined by the situation, and violating the 5-7 Rule for member size becomes a necessity at times. For example, I was involved in an industrial factory with a future project. Project scope was extensive and carried through four phases over a five year planning and implementation period. The four phases were required due to timing of capital availability and practical limitations on the organization's ability to manage mega-change. Several committees, teams, and sub-teams were involved in the process. Some of the action teams exceeded a dozen members - one or two approaching twenty members.

What situation justified this large team size and apparent violation of the 5-7 Rule? The main issues were that the long term survival of the business required a quality decision and approach; and, of equal importance, we needed a buy-in and subsequent agreement by all interested parties as well.

The situation being that unilateral action by management was not desirable, feasible, or possible. Rank and file were represented by three bargaining units with existing contract agreements binding on all.

Involving workers from all operations in the team process surprisingly did not slow the process one whit. The time spent up-front in investigation and dialogue sharply reduced the implementation time at the back end. In addition, there were no instant surprises or shock waves to deliver to the rank and file once decisions were made. They were involved through the process and team members communicated their concurrence down through their fellow workers.

| FRAME CELL PROJECT TEAM | | |
|---|---|---|
| **TEAM MEMBER** | **SOURCE DEPARTMENT** | **FUNCTION** |
| Tom | Fabrication | Chair |
| Slim | Supervision | Owner |
| Willie | Welding | End User |
| Robert | Structural | End User |
| Clifford | Production | Expertise |
| Dave | Engineering | Expertise |
| Jay | Maintenance | Expertise |
| Joe | Methods | Core Group |

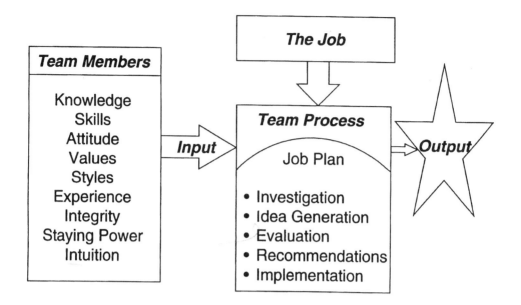

**Team Members**

Knowledge
Skills
Attitude
Values
Styles
Experience
Integrity
Staying Power
Intuition

**The Job**

**Input**

**Team Process**

Job Plan

- Investigation
- Idea Generation
- Evaluation
- Recommendations
- Implementation

**Output**

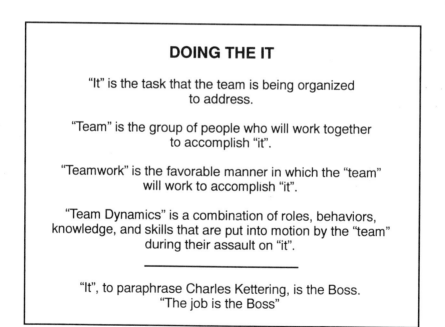

## DOING THE IT

"It" is the task that the team is being organized
to address.

"Team" is the group of people who will work together
to accomplish "it".

"Teamwork" is the favorable manner in which the "team"
will work to accomplish "it".

"Team Dynamics" is a combination of roles, behaviors,
knowledge, and skills that are put into motion by the "team"
during their assault on "it".

---

"It", to paraphrase Charles Kettering, is the Boss.
"The job is the Boss"

# CHAPTER FOUR
## NATURE OF TEAMS

### MAKING OF A TEAM

### The Making Of A Team: Selecting the Right Members

In building a team it is necessary to select the right people for the task to be performed. Who are the right people:

> No General can fight his battles alone, He must depend on his lieutenants, and his success depends on his ability to select the right man for the right place.
>
> *– J. Ogden Armour*

We can learn something about team principles by taking a look at a cake baking process. Once the baker decides on what the product will be, then she/he goes about selecting the right ingredients, the correct proportions, guided by a recipe, and the sequence to be followed.

Too much sugar will fail a cake just as well as too much salt.

And the ingredients are far different if one has decided on a banana cake rather than angel food.

The team process is much analogous to baking a cake. An objective is considered, team members selected who participate appropriately, a process ensues, and an outcome prevails.

In selecting prospective team members, there is seldom a one all right team; rather, particularly in larger organizations, there is an array of combinations that might prove worthy.

The urgency of the task is one issue; is there time to bring a team along that might currently not be fully proficient, but has great potential?

I'm reminded of fifth graders entering the music world by acquiring their first instrument. Their objective is to play music and be a part of the high school band. Assembled together as a band, they are not competent in the early going; as well understood. The notes sometimes resemble barnyard noises.

To have competence, A. Chickering in his Fork of Competency concept suggests that one must have a triad of knowledge, skills, and attitude. Certainly, the beginning musicians had but one ingredient at the start; but an essential one – attitude. Knowledge and skills would come through hard work and continued practice.

Similarly, team members should also be selected on the basis of matched knowledge, skills, and attitudes that could be marshaled to handle the task being considered.

Nonetheless, teams require another essential element as well. And that, importantly, is to be able to work together with colleagues on a team in a manner that engenders success.

> *The secret is to work less as individuals and more as a team. As a coach, I play not my eleven best, but my best eleven.*
> *– Knute Rockne*

## Women Participation On Industrial Teams:

Having three daughters and a lovely wife has made me sensitive to the issues surrounding female participation in the workplace.

Regarding participation of females on teams familiar to me, I would assess their performance as entirely equal and similar to male counterparts; a cut above average in most cases.

If anything in team interaction changes with mixed gender teams, I think it is that males tend to show off a little bit more at first; and rougher language by some spirited individuals tones down, as well it should.

Acceptance of female counterparts by male team members seems no problem, and the earlier patronizing, without intent, seems to have disappeared with time. They are equals.

There is yet a shortfall of female employees holding industrial management positions in traditional male functions such as Engineering; consequently, the pool for selecting female team members from the functions is currently somewhat limited.

It is up to the team leader to see that assignments are not made that seem gender based. For example, I recall an early team where the female member was always assigned to the role of secretary. Not by chance, but by conscious decision that this indeed was a job native to her talents.

This was demeaning in that she was probably the top intellect on the team and would have contributed much more active participation if not being busily occupied scribbling meeting notes.

28

There is not much more to say about this subject from my point of view, except to reinforce the fact that gender should be transparent in selecting capable team members.

Variety is the spice of life they say, and a mix of gender, age and experience adds much to the colorful makeup of a team, and gives it life.

## Age as a Factor in Team Member Performance

There are differing opinions about the effect of a team member's age in the group dynamics process.

With good reason.

It does make a difference; but when, how, and in what mix? Largely, it depends upon what the team's task is all about. If the issue is a professional sports team, then, except for a Cal Ripken or a George Blanda, forty-ish is about the high side limit. Unfortunately, it is a fact of life that you cannot run as fast, throw as far, or lift as much as the aging process occurs. Few would argue this point. So, age is a legitimate factor in assembling a physically demanding sports team. Yet, how many coaches or team trainers do you find without some speckled patches of gray in their hair? Not many, and coaches are as much true team members of a team as are the players. What this suggests is that teams can and do function well with a mix of ages and talents on a team.

Teams organized in business settings and volunteer organizations are a different matter. Rather than physical stamina, knowledge, skills, initiative, and attitude become the prime factors in team member selection. This could mean a team with a hybrid mix of ages.

Consider the make-up of various teams or councils in non-profit organizations. Often, the team consists of the paid staff along with volunteer retired business executives residing in the community. Given the wealth of their professional business experience, free of a vested interest, the retirees bring great capability to the team.

Nevertheless, there is a stereotyped notion of characteristics associated with a prospective team member's age. Clichés and adages abound.

"Experience is the best teacher," favoring maturity.

"You can't teach an old dog new tricks," chalk one up for the younger player.

"A person can be old at twenty, or young at eighty; it's largely a personal choice." A dead heat.

But performance by the age mix of teams is not governed by adages or generalized perceptions.

## PERCEIVED CHARACTERISTICS BY AGE

| YOUNGER | OLDER |
|---------|-------|
| **CONTINUUM** | |

| | |
|---|---|
| ENERGY | WISDOM |
| INNOCENCE | EXPERIENCE |
| RISK TAKERS | STABILITY |
| CREATIVE | PATIENT |
| AMBITIOUS | NURTURING |
| TECHNOLOGY | PRACTICALITY |

Scientific data and replicated studies on the effect of age mix on teams is hard to come by; there are just too many variables involved. However, through empirical observations over time, it is possible to arrive at some pretty realistic expectations.

- Team Spirit
  Just as mixed genders adds spirit and vitality to a team, so does a mixture of ages. Rather than being apples alike, an age imbalance brings varied perspectives and experiences.

- Wisdom and Experience
  While it is possible that there is nothing like an old fool, it is unlikely that an old fool would be a candidate for team membership. For wisdom and experience, give the edge to age.

- Open Mindedness
  Probably an edge to younger team members. They are not as battle scarred nor likely to have as much turf or status to protect. Depending upon how one views it, a junior employee may be either naive or more receptive to a particular idea that has been deep sixed a dozen times before. Senior members are more prone to play the "we tried that before; didn't work" tape.

- Youthful Energy and Enthusiasm
  The euphemism featuring the energy and enthusiasm of youth is largely correct. Look all around if you have any doubts. However, a cautioning note. Many

individuals carry tremendous energy throughout even the golden years of life. Energy is not a private characteristic of the younger set.

- Cooperation versus Competition Among Team Members
  A cooperative mode of operation usually accompanies a team consisting of mixed age membership. Mutual trust is particularly enhanced if personal values such as respect for elders and a nurturing bent toward junior members prevail. A negative effect, if any exists, usually is confined to a relationship between two specific individuals. Rather than disharmony being an age issue, it usually is associated with personality types. A younger lion may be seen as impudent and brash; an older lion may be seen as protective of turf and status. Either way it should be remembered that lions of equal age do not always team well together either.

Summarizing the empirical experience, I would have no hesitation in composing a hybrid team consisting of mixed ages, genders, and length of service in the organization.

## Beware the Team Member with Vested Interests

When structuring the matrix make-up of a team, the job is often the boss. Rather than selecting team members by virtue of their talents or attitudes, appointments are often dictated by who holds a particular position. For example, if you were organizing an industrial make versus buy evaluation team, you would probably want multi-functional representation consisting of a Buyer, Methods Engineer, and Accountant and, perhaps someone from Quality Assurance; or something akin to that. Your people choices may well be limited; particularly if lone individuals filled those vital functions.

This situation could well leave you with a potential member who has deep personal interests in the outcome. Their authority or position could be threatened. Options available to a team leader may be one of selecting the lesser of two evils. Having a team member who stonewalls the initiative and drives the process to a self indulged conclusion; or excluding this particular member, whose function is key, and having to deal with him later in the decision process at which time with a back against the wall and sandbags in front, he may well have fortified the position deflecting all proposals.

Many teams have felt the passions of this dilemma and wrestled with how to deal with it. To understand the underlying reasons for the vested interests a member might hold, betraying objectivity, one only need look at some poignant examples of real life situations. Here are some.

- The general manager has formed a team to consider integrating the design engineering and industrial engineering functions. Does it make sense to include both the chief industrial engineer and the director of engineering on this team – when its pretty obvious that one big fish will probably prevail upon restructuring? And what if one or both are excluded from the process? How well will the outcome suggested by others be accepted? The same analogy would fit a department or grocery store if contemplating integration of merchandising functions.

- Seeking to downsize the warehousing function in all respects; storage, logistics and personnel, a team is organized to investigate just-in-time concepts. Do you welcome the warehouse manager as an integral, objective member of the team?

Implementation could mean less authority, fewer employees, and maybe a lower job position.

- Recognizing the significant costs of maintaining your company's fleet, should you request your truck driver's participation on a team to examine common carriers as an alternate choice?

- Examining the pink paint of the ceilings and walls of your offices and hallways, you contemplate fielding a team of internal maintenance people to examine the merits of subcontracting the painting to outside contractors.

- During a reengineering effort, you get the notion that perhaps expediting is a non-value added function. How about organizing a team which will include a couple of savvy expediters and their boss to work on the issue? If successful, the former expediters could join the lemmings in marching off the White Cliffs of Dover singing, "*Stout Hearted Men*".

Chances of individuals being dispassionate and completely objective in sensitive matters, rival that of getting my dinner date with Sharon Stone; albeit her hometown is only about thirty miles distant.

These situations are not uncommon in business organizations. Human beings, as much as dogs and deer in the Animal Kingdom, tend to be territorial-turf protective and have nurturing and survival instincts.

But the saving grace is that humans possess an overwhelming capability to reason. If individuals, call them employees here, enjoy mutual trust and respect with employers, then uncertainties will be dealt with and altruism and objectivity will prevail.

Experience implores us to include – not exclude – those individuals on a team who can contribute to the process improvements, despite some measure of apprehension. It is far better to include them during the team's deliberations than face the possibility of a broadside later in the decision and implementation process.

During the heydays when the Pittsburgh Steeler Football Team reigned supreme, the former Houston Oilers were also not a half bad team. Their biggest problem was living in the same decade as the Steelers. I will never forget how Houston's Head Coach Bum Phillips responded when a sports reporter asked him about the Oilers chances one year. He said, "The road to the Superbowl goes through Pittsburgh."

What he meant was that the Steelers would have to be dealt with. There was no avoiding them. I think this theme is perfectly analogous to including team members from important areas who may be holding vested interests. You must deal with the issues sooner or later; sooner the better. Invite them in as valued, trusted members. If the organization's character and values are well founded, the outcome is usually a good one.

## New Teams: Getting Off On The Right Track

It is not uncommon that you will find yourself as the designated leader of a team whose assignment is defined, and participants already selected.

Continuing this scenario, my experience has been that seldom will you have the luxury of a veteran, well oiled team who harmoniously worked together many times before.

Further, on occasion, one or more team members might be assigned full time to the project; however, the reality is that, in most circumstances, team members are expected to participate on a part time basis, while performing their current job as well.

It doesn't matter which case applies, as this discussion applies equally well to both conditions, full or part time. Also, the variables such as might be introduced by including global colleagues or suppliers as internal team members is embraced by the following discussions as well.

## Paramount Rule #1

You, as the team leader, must get a good read on your resources very early in the group dynamics process if you are to succeed.

### Case Study: Team Project Involving Customer And Supplier
Early in my career, I was appointed as team leader of a Value Engineering project to reduce costs on a high cost purchased item used in our products. The make-up of the assembled team was to include six members from the supplier's organization and an equal number from our company. It was to be a joint effort with mutual benefit; lower cost for us, more potential volume for them.

The objective was to reduce product price by fifteen percent; an objective not all that thrilling to the supplier, incidentally. But, the supplier was driven to cooperate fully as cost relief was imperative. To date, they alone had not provided any.

The situation was compromised somewhat by the fact that the week long team meeting was slated to be held mid-way between our distant facilities at a modest hotel. Except for knowing the position, titles, and functions that would be represented by the supplier, little was known about their key players.

Looking at those bodies assembled at the opening session, I could only imagine the degree of expertise, interpersonal skills, and initiative that laid behind the limpid pools and hope for the best.

Who among the team would be helpful?
Would they open up? All of them?
How free would they be with their internal cost data?
Who might be wishing away the time, praying for Friday to come?
A tough situation to be sure, fraught with uncertainty.

Well, the good news is that a skilled leader can greatly influence the probability of a successful outcome. Here's one approach that's worked for me in getting a good read on participants and making adjustments as necessary to engender success.

First, think about what could go wrong in later team meetings that might jeopardize the process; then apply some preventative medicine up front to minimize those detractors.

## Detractors and Counter Remedies
    I.   Idea Killers
    II.  Rush to Judgment
    III. Ego Centered Behavior
    IV. Lop Sided Communication

## I. Idea Killers and the Remedy

Overly negative reaction by team members to another's ideas, concepts, or recommendations by others is potentially damaging. There are serious consequences as a result of heavy put downs; among them perhaps a reluctance by the idea person to offer other input. Further, there is always the likelihood of revenge; as you did not like my idea, conversely, all ideas you present to me will be judged to suck, also. The one-upsmanship will continue.

> *Creativity is so delicate a flower that praise tends to make it bloom while discouragement often nips it in the bud.*
>
> *—Thomas Carlyle*

To mitigate negative reactions later, consider conducting a brainstorming exercise up front. This exercise, properly run, will serve three purposes:

A.  An ice breaker which gets team members talking and participating; something akin to morning calisthenics of the mind.

B.  Provides an idea generating technique that they can use in later team processes and use it correctly.

C.  Importantly, the Defer Judgment Principle becomes ingrained in their current thinking.

This investment in time up front in the team process will return great dividends later.

## II. Rush to Judgment and the Remedy

Americans, in particular, have a rugged individualist can-do attitude. This is good and this is bad. On the downside, and, perhaps at one extreme, there is a tendency to try to solve a problem before knowing what the question is. A built-in impatience.

No matter what project a team is working on, information gathering is always one of the phases. Historically, if there has been one phase of the job plan or project that is most neglected, it is the information gathering phase. Training in gathering information has often been limited to the simple statement – "Get the facts; Get all the facts".

More is needed.

Complicating the process, team members will, at times, hold honest wrong beliefs going into a project which will not be challenged or tested during team processing. Because of the held belief, not known to be wrong, the information will be presented as gospel and acted upon as such.

So, you have an issue here; a rush to judgment abetted sometimes by honest wrong beliefs. How to preclude these detractors from unduly effecting team processing during the life of the team? Here is one technique I use called 'The World's Easiest Quiz'.

Good natured, it starts out normally with the team snickering, but, all in all, having some fun. The sequence goes something like this:

1. Who was buried in Grant's tomb?
   Collectively, the team says – "Grant".

2. In what country did India Ink originate?
   Collectively, all answer – "India". No – it was Persia.

3. In what state was the Kentucky Rifle made?
   Most say – "Kentucky"; a couple say – "Pennsylvania".
   Pennsylvania is the correct answer; to which a couple of team
   members will ask, "Why?"

4. Atop what hill did the Battle of Bunker Hill take place?
   A few good students of American History will correctly know it was
   Breed's Hill. (Bunker Hill being an honest wrong belief held by
   some early colonists).

5. How long did the Hundred Years War last?
   Only a couple of team members will say – "100 years".
   The remaining team members, becoming slightly frustrated,
   embarrassed, or cautious will utter nothing.

6. How long did the Thirty Years War last?
   By this time, almost no one will offer thirty years as an answer which,
   incidentally, is the correct answer. Instead, they will jocularly guess –
   "thirty-two, thirty-three, thirty-four years and two months", etc...

And so on down through the remaining questions. By the time the team hears the last question – "What color was George Washington's horse 'Whitey'", they are responding with crazed replies of "pinto, roan, appaloosa, black", etc...

At this point, we discuss the point being made by the exercise. That is, going into a project, it is natural to hold some preconceived ideas or long held beliefs that may no longer be correct. We need to consciously examine the data, opinions, or what we view as facts germane to the project without rushing to judgment early.

## III. Ego Centered Behavior and a Remedy

A strong ego is not bad. It is a constraint, however, in team building when one member holds an overly optimistic value of his/her capability, while seeing little merit in that of fellow members. At extremes, it is an attitude reflecting, "I'm Okay – Nobody else is quite Okay".

These personality types can be quite a contributor to the team if only the energy and confidence they exhibit can be channeled into productive efforts.

An exercise that I favor early in the team building process is one that demonstrates the value of a team, which normally and almost always supersedes the possibilities of an individual working alone.

One such exercise I use, and there are others, is called "American Inventors" which was originally discovered on a placemat in a restaurant. The exercise features a dozen questions inquiring what inventor was responsible for certain inventions. A three step process is used in attempting to make valid points relating to team activities. In the first phase, the individuals act alone in attempting to provide answers to the questions. Five minutes is allowed for this purpose. Although possible, never have I found that a team member, acting alone, knows all the correct answers. Since memory alone, if indeed an individual had been exposed to the knowledge earlier, is the basis for an answer, little is to be gained by extending the time limit. Normally, a person is stuck after just a minute or two.

Secondly, I then instruct the members to act as a team in confronting the questions. Another five minutes is allocated for this joint exercise. At this point, it is not often that, even with team input, all answers are forthcoming correctly.

Finally, keeping the teams together, I distribute a list of the a list of the actual inventors in random order to match up with the inventions. Following this added information, the teams generally arrive at the correct answers or, failing that, don't miss by much.

Points being made by this exercise which bear on team activities:

- A team working together normally has better, more complete knowledge than one of the same individuals working alone.

- A team unsure of certain pieces of information, rather than guesses, should consult with, or determine where correct data might be found.

## Lopsided Communication

Some team members may be overly talkative, while others may be shy and reluctant to verbalize their opinions and feelings. A good start at the initial team meeting goes a long way toward setting the tone for future meetings.

A round table self introduction of team members, relating their background and experiences, builds some esteem and understanding early in the team building process.

A timid person is as much a challenge as a loquacious one. In each case, the team leader and/or adept fellow team members can do much to improve the situation.

Shy people can be included by requesting written input, asking questions directly of a person, and early on seizing every opportunity to build trust with the individual.

Techniques such as Brainwriting, Crawford Slip Writing, and Nominal Group Technique are good ways to include team members' input who are reluctant to articulate their thoughts.

# CHAPTER FIVE
## TEAM BUILDING

The question – "How to build a team?" is much like asking is it better to live in the city or in the country. The answer could be nonsensical unless you knew what kind of a team one was talking about.

How does a tone deaf youngster, aspiring to become a musician, eventually become one? Some ingredients that come quickly to mind are a learned knowledge of music, training under a maestro, harmony with other musicians, an attitude, and practice, practice, practice. Some of the very same traits are common to the aspiring team members.

I view the team building process as consisting of four basic cornerstones, each having four strong elements. These may be considered the 4x4's of the team building process.

## I. Knowledge

All people bring with them to the job, high levels of knowledge which, technically speaking, becomes dated over time.

The Keuffel and Esser Slide Rule lying dormant in my desk drawer is a constant reminder of that. It matters not that my deftness and expertise in its use brought applause from my college classmates. It is now I who tread the keyboards like Columbus, searching for a key, while younger colleagues rapidly pound their laptops.

Knowledge is key for team members. Consequently, it is a most important part of the team building process. Team members are selected, in large part, for the expertise they can bring to the team in a given area. Since few of us have expertise in all areas, it is necessary to have at least one participating member expert in various facets of the study.

To acquire knowledge on a continuing basis is a noble goal. To remain competitive in a global marketplace, it is absolutely essential.

Responsibility for providing a learning opportunity lies both with the organization and with the individual. Ongoing opportunities for learning include the following four:

1. On site company sponsored training programs

2. External seminars and conferences
3. Self instruction courses and improvement
4. Benchmarking.

Some organizations are greatly committed to employee training programs; others, sadly, are not, downsizing their offerings as a means to preserve funds. This is risky business if continued on the long run.

Conventional wisdom says it correctly: "If you think education is expensive, try ignorance".

Summarizing the first point in building a team – Knowledge. Knowledge is power. Knowledge is an important ingredient in the team building process.

## II. Skill Sets

It is helpful to think of skill sets as the tools which multiply the effect of the knowledge team members possess.

Looking forward into the group dynamics that will occur during the team process, ask yourself these questions:

- What skills will the team members need to address the issues that will arise?
- What special skills will the team need to deal with abstract issues and the unknown.
- What skills will enable the team to work effectively and in harmony?

Skills have more to do with how you do something, the method employed, rather than expertise in technical areas.

Four key skills that are needed in the team process are:

1. Problem Solving
2. Interpersonal
3. Communication
4. Decision Making

Knowing that these four skills complement the team process, specific training must address these areas. It is strategic to think in terms of upfront training of potential team members prior to being selected for a particular team project.

Taking a page out of Louie Pasteur's book, "Success Comes to Those with the Prepared Mind". Failing that pre-training, mini-courses can be conducted concurrently as the project moves on.

A benefit of team members having similar training in techniques and skills is that all will understand the language, concepts, and techniques that will be used throughout the team project.

# TEAM BUILDING

> A benefit of team members having similar training in techniques and skills is that all will understand the language, concepts, and techniques that will be used throughout the team project

## 1. Problem Solving Skills Training Programs

A. Problem Solving
B. Problem Identification
C. Problem Solving by Objectives
D. Synectics

E. Is-Is Not Logic
F. Logic Diagraming
G. Reality Brainstorming
H. Attribute Comparison Techniques

## 2. Interpersonal Skills Training

A. Conflict Resolution
B. Negotiation Tactics
C. Timing Issues

One such timing issue is knowing the appropriate time to defer judgment on table issues. The ability to defer judgment on a colleague's idea or proposal is a valued trait. Sometimes, the temptation to react unfavorably or kill an idea is strong – and maybe the idea does stink; but, in the interest of sensitivity and respect for a team member's feelings the urge should be throttled. After all, if the individual did not think it was a promising idea, it wouldn't have been brought forth.

Practicing the classical rules of brainstorming by Alex Osborn will assure that the Defer Judgment Principle will be considered during the team process.

> **Classical Brainstorming Rules**
> - Team Effort
> - Free Wheeling
> - Defer Judgment
> - Force Ideas
> - Hitchhike on Other's Ideas

## 3. Communication Skills

There is an array of programs available to sharpen a team member's communication skills. They range from informal dialogue to public speaking, to listening skills.

Special attention must be given to the written communications that are an essential part of the ongoing team process. Major documents are:

- Meeting Minutes
- Meeting Agendas
- Action Plans
- Progress Reports
- Final Reports

Communications beyond the team reaching out to interested parties in the rest of the organization, is most important. Ordinarily, the work that a team is doing will impact the organization; otherwise, it is doubtful that a team would have been involved. While it is not necessary to communicate chapter and verse of all detailed happenings, salient points should be periodically forwarded. Remember that decision makers do not particularly like surprises during a final team presentation. Unwelcome news may well be met with a conditioned negative response.

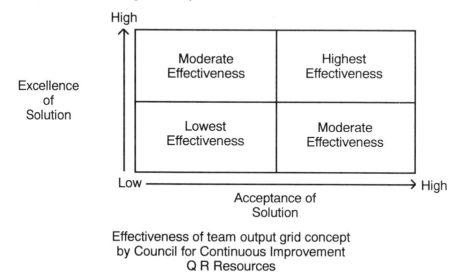

Effectiveness of team output grid concept
by Council for Continuous Improvement
Q R Resources

## 4. Decision Making Skills

Educational programs that will sharpen a team member's skills in decision making follows:

1. Numerical Evaluation of Alternatives
2. Risk Analysis
3. Pareto Analysis
4. Force Field Analysis

Summarizing the four key points of skill sets. Team members skills will be greatly improved through educational training programs in the areas of:

- Problem Solving
- Interpersonal Skills
- Communication Skills
- Decision Making

## III. Attitude

Team members must be competent in order to be significant contributors to the task at hand. The fork of competency concept as developed by A. Chickering, has attitude as one of the three fork tines: knowledge and skills being the others.

Attitude is important. Attitude has to do with mental state: how we feel about things which, in turn, tend to make us act in a certain behavior. Our attitude influences our behavior to participate; or, withdraw from the team process. Our attitude influences our behavior to energetically plow new ground or withhold services.

One phenomenon about attitude that has become absolutely clear is this: a good attitude which was cultivated over many years can be severely damaged by thought-lessness, seemingly, in nanoseconds.

This book is not the forum for elaborating deeply on this subject except to note that it is one of the great failings prevalent in management today.

Four important elements that are contained within attitude are:

1. A Felt Freedom to Act
2. Self Esteem
3. Positive Attitude
4. Ability to Shrug off Adversity

## 1. Felt Freedom to Act

Today the buzzword is empowerment. And, the connotation is that upper manage-ment suddenly seizes an opportunity to tell their team subordinates – go for it. The fact is that members of high performance teams have always acted in that manner. These star performers have always felt freedom to act. Delivering success, these hi-perfor-mance types were always accorded a measure of autonomy by superiors. Peter Uberroth made a profound statement: "Authority is 20 percent given and 80 percent taken".

## 2. Self Esteem

Self Esteem is contagious and has a confidence building effort of the team at large.

## 3. Positive Attitude

A positive attitude is universally known as a favorable attribute. Ross Perot said it as well as anybody: "When building a team, I always search first for people who love to win. If I can't find any of those, I look for people who hate to lose."

## 4. Ability to Shrug off Adversity

Every dog has his day; and, every dog has a bad day once in a while. In order to maintain a healthy attitude, it is necessary to maintain a well modulated composure. Fellow team members admire colleagues who can maintain their composure in stress-ful times.

# IV. Working Together

The manner in which the team works together is dependent upon the style and tempo of the team. There are four important aspects of working together, being:

1. Informal Team Rules
2. Mutual Respect

3. Mutual Trust
4. Enjoyable Time Together

1. Informal Team Rules

Ground rules are a good idea provided that the team does not go overboard with their zeal. Ground rules should be simple: many of which should be assumed or established by prior training or team participation. Some basic rules that apply are:

- Meeting attendance is critical. Consensus on whether substitute members are an acceptable option.
- Meeting logistics: agreement on meeting times, duration, frequency, and location.
- Full participation and active team support

If the team activity is part-time, the proper balance must be maintained between a member's primary job and the team project.

2. Mutual Respect

If the team is operating together for the first time, warm-up exercises are in order. This would include a self-introductory of members, highlighting their background experiences and talents they bring to the party.

One way to cultivate mutual respect, particularly in appreciating others ideas, is the idea advocate technique. Following the team members input of ideas, each idea is randomly assigned to a member to act as an advocate for the idea. In this way, every idea will have a chance at a fair hearing.

3. Mutual Trust

Trust is a straightforward issue. Team members should be predictable in a solid way. Say what you will do: do what you say. Douglas McGregor, in elaborating on trust issues, said, "I know you will not take unfair advantage of me. It also means that I can put my status and self esteem in this group or relationship and my career in your hands with complete confidence". That trust, in fellow team members, is certainly on the high side of altruism these days; but, it does speak to the nobler side of trust.

4. Celebration

It is important for the team to have an enjoyable time together. A fun experience is needed to build cohesiveness and energize the team. If the meetings and subsequent assignments become a drudge, frustration sets in. Frustration begets blame. To inject life into a team, small wins and successes should be cause for celebration. Also, varying the meeting sites and inviting ad hoc members to participate from time to time works well also.

If, in your upbringing, you thought it immodest to celebrate successes within a team setting, be assured times have changed. One only need to view sports teams antics on a Sunday afternoon to verify the transition. Spectators are amused at the antics: high five's, butt slapping, hugging, dancing, and occasionally immersing one's self in the crowd. So, celebrate a little.

Summarizing the 4x4's of Building a Team

| FOUR CORNERSTONES | | | |
|---|---|---|---|
| KNOWLEDGE | SKILLS | ATTITUDE | WORKING TOGETHER |
| On-Site Training | Problem Solving | Freedom to Act | Team Rules |
| Seminars | Interpersonal | Self Esteem | Mutual Respect |
| Self Learning | Communication | Positive Attitude | Mutual Trust |
| Benchmarking | Decision Making | Shrug off Adversity | Celebration |

## A TEAM WITH TOOLS

Much is made about motivation and its impact on performances. Much is made about attitude, and well it should. But, what I feel has really been shortshrifted in team-work is the emphasis on proper tools.

Tools and methods are the multiplier of the human input. Who would argue with the fact that a midget with a chainsaw could out-produce Paul Bunyan with his legendary ax? Tools make the difference.

An unhappy woman with a bulldozer can outproduce the happiest of men armed with a shovel. Tools make a big difference.

The tools we are talking about in team efforts are the various techniques that can be used during the team dynamics process. Different techniques that apply to various phases of a systematic job plan follow, but is not meant to be construed as a full listing.

- Information Gathering
  - Situation Analysis      Attribute Comparison Techniques (ACT)
  - Is/Is Not Logic      Redundancy Analysis Techniques (RAT)
  - Pareto Analysis      Software Analysis Techniques (SAT)
  - Cost Visibility      Cost Driver Analysis
  - Cost Charting      Logic Diagraming

- Idea Generation
  - Brainstorming      Gordon Technique
  - Synetics      Stop & Go Brainstorming
  - Idea Matrices      Reality Brainstorming

- **Evaluation**
  - Numerical Evaluation      Project Evaluation Techniques (PET)
  - Combinex      Potential Problem Analysis (PPA)
  - Paired Comparisons      Nominal Group Techniques (NGT)
  - Risk Analysis      Fault-tree Analysis

- Implementation
  - Force Field Analysis

# SYSTEMATIC APPROACH IS PARAMOUNT

The most noticeable ingredient missing from inexperienced teams, to a trained eye, is the conscious following of a systematic plan. Without a concept in mind, the team dialogue often meanders back and forth like a person trapped in a house of mirrors.

To progress, the team needs to know where it is going and how to get there. It is not necessary that all teams follow exactly the same plan. That wouldn't work. Not only are organizational cultures and styles different, but the nature of the tasks as well. One wouldn't expect to attack a hardware project in the same manner as a software one, nor the modification of a proven product versus a pie in the sky think tank project. They are dissimilar animals.

But, there are some universal truths: in any team project, four elements will remain constant in a lockstep sequence, following each other in turn. They are: information gathering, idea generation, evaluation, and implementation. Obviously, evaluation should not precede idea generation, and idea generation should not occur until the upfront information is in and the situation determined. Keep in mind that the idea generation phase is creative and free wheeling. As such, it should not be mixed with the serious (adult) business of gather data, nor the parental ego state so prevalent in the evaluation phase.

| Conventional Problem Solving | Value Engineering Job Plan |
|---|---|
| 1. Define the problem | 1. Information Gathering |
| 2. Generate ideas for solving. | 2. Function Analysis |
| | 3. Creativity Phase |
| 3. Refine the ideas and select. | 4. Analytical Phase |
| 4. Implement the solution. | 5. Implementation |

## TEAM BUILDING SKILLS

| COGNITIVE | AFFECTIVE |
|---|---|
| • Evaluation<br>• Synthesis<br>• Analysis<br>• Application<br>• Comprehension<br>• Knowledge | • Self-Control<br>• Caring<br>• Responding<br>• Receiving<br>• Characterizing<br>• Organizing<br>• Valuing |

# CHAPTER SIX
## TEAM DYNAMICS

Team Dynamics as expressed here is the manner in which the team members interact as the process moves forward. Essentially, it is the impressions that an astute observer might get from observing team happenings through a one way mirror. Inherent in the team dynamics would the the nature of the participation, conflict, urgency, styles of influence and leadership, groupthink, morale and other ingredients in the process.

Unless some of the team members have worked together on teams before, some sizing up of each others values will occur. Clock time is essential. Trust will be earned over time, rarely bestowed at the onset. Some tips in getting started under these conditions follow.

### Goal clarity:
Start the meeting with a clear understanding of what the objective is. What war you are fighting, with whom, what your resources are, and what victory might look like.

### Respect for individuality within the team:
Self introduction of team members highlighting their special skills, experience and background information.

### Steer through icebergs ahead:
By consensus, establish mutually favorable meeting times, dates, frequency and length of meetings.

### Informally build trust:
Set tone for Modus Operandi by emphasizing the open, candid interaction desired and the need for patience in deferring judgment and heavy criticism on sensitive issues.

## Factors In Team Success

1. The assignment is valid and worthy

2. Selected members have necessary capability.

3. The members understand and agree with the assignment.

4. The members derive satisfaction from participation.

5. The team is well accepted externally.

6. Members have a healthy level of frustration.

7. The team performs to expectations.

8. The team has a sense of humor.

9. The team size is limited – usually 5-7 members for normal duties.

10. Allowance is made for handling their regular job functions.

## Contractual Agreements Among Team Members

The concept of drawing up formal contracts among individuals or teams is foreign to me. Call me an agnostic regarding the value of contracts, written or oral, among team members. Just as raw oysters do not appeal to some, while others shuck them by the bushel, so my adverse feelings for contracts in informal teams and relationships. I do not find them advantageous.

I'm certain that my upbringing had a lot to do with this light perception of contracts. Family values meant everything to my parents. Plain folks, my father a farmer/miner, my mother a teacher/homemaker, advocated mutual trust, deferring to a promise, a handshake, and a person's word in lieu of the need for a formal contract.

The exceptions would be in instances dictated by formal cash transactions such as buying or renting a home. Obviously, a formal, legally binding contract is called for here.

In lieu of                    or some upfront discussion among team members, settling
on                            amework for working together.

s

and written about the various roles team members play
have been identified.

possibilities, nearly all teams openly feature only two
Leader or Chair and a Secretary who records and
'ler groups, the leader often assumes the secretary

Nevertheless, team members do assume and take on individual roles on their own volition as evidenced by their behavior or special talents. But this is done by personal choice or inclination. It has seldom been my experience that a team leader will specifically charge a particular member to assume the role of "Clarifier", or "Mediator", "Sergeant-at-Arms", or the like.

Another point to make is that individual members can well take on multiple behavior roles, or what might be seen as some overlapping roles by other fellow team members.

A role such as expert in a particular functional area is largely self-evident. For example, if an accountant exists on the team, it is likely that she would be looked to for expertise in that area; likewise, a metallurgist would be looked to for expertise relating to material properties in metals.

## COLLAGE OF VARIOUS TEAMS ROLES AS DESCRIBED BY MANY OVER THE YEARS. CAN YOU ADD TO THE LIST?

| | | | |
|---|---|---|---|
| Leader | Secretary | Telephoner | Blocker |
| Chair | Expert | Info Gatherer | Dominator |
| Facilitator | Compromiser | Gatekeeper | Opponent |
| Dazzler | Clarifier | Investigator | Idea Person |
| Moderator | Advocate | Summarizer | Devil's Advocate |
| Harmonizer | Gopher | Consensus Seeker | Orienter |
| Elaborator | Coordinator | Energizer | Recorder |
| Recorder | Follower | Playboy | Presenter |
| Catalyst | Rescuer | Scheduler | Critical Advocate |

The fascination of teams is greatly enriched by the interesting combinations of team members and the skills and personality they bring to the party.

It comes as no surprise that certain team members will be more nurturing and benevolent; while others may be seen as cold and impersonal.

## TEAM MEMBER ROLES BY CATEGORY TYPE

| FACILITATION | INTERPERSONAL SKILLS | FUNCTIONS AND TASKS | DRIVERS | DETRACTORS |
|---|---|---|---|---|
| Chair | Advocate | Secretary | Catalyst | Dazzler |
| Clarifier | Harmonizer | Recorder | Idea Person | Road Blocker |
| Consensus Seeker | Mediator | Gophers | Free Spirit | Dominator |
| Compromiser | Devil's Advocate | Knowledge Experts | Energizer | Malcontent |

Using some imagination, the multitude of expressed roles can be classified into categorical types; one possibility is the categories of facilitation, interpersonal skills, function, drivers, and detractors.

# TEAM MEMBER ROLES:

Obviously, all team members have a role; otherwise they would not be members of the team. Some roles however, are more formally defined than others.

The more prominent role names are leader and secretary. Other role names ascribed to certain team members such as mediator, expert, and devils advocate are a product of their particular behavior rather than an assigned role.

The leader is normally the most crucial position on the team. Just being the leader, he/she is usually given respect and listened up to in meetings, calling the shots, moving things forward, assigning work, scheduling meetings and providing communication outside the teams. I think it is safe to say that few team members are held as accountable for the success and outcome of the teamwork as the leader.

The team leadership role has changed dramatically in recent times; for one thing, the name has evolved in many circles from chairman, to chair, to leader and often now as facilitator.

## Team Leader

The individual in a leadership role on a team is called by a variety of terms. A few are chair, leader, or facilitator. Does a team have to have a leader? It seems so. For one reason, it's always been that way. Probably a throwback to early military or religious hierarchies.

Incidentally, have you ever known of a football team where the tightend called the offensive plays? No, it's always the quarterback with help from the sidelines.

The distinction of a quarterback, or leader, on a business team is not so clear. It is likely that the team may have been organized without a formal leader being named at the onset. No matter – whether or not one is appointed, one will emerge.

More and more, we find, in team functioning today, that the leader chosen is not necessarily the brightest, strongest, or highest status member on the team. Practicality seems to have over-ridden egos in today's management team.

People are more comfortable with a matrix style management today: at least in part this seems due to flatter organizations and more experience and comfort levels with teams. All team members share responsibility for much of the happenings during the group dynamics process – the outcome or results being primary. All have a duty to provide input, challenge assumptions, and follow up on assignments. All are responsible for maintaining acceptable behavior and perhaps acting as mediators and rescuers if situations warrant.

Despite all of this shared accountability, however, the yoke ordinarily falls heaviest on the leader (or chair). There are tasks which, if not the sole responsibility of the leader, by degree, point heavily in that direction. The chart following lists many of these.

The good leader is neither overbearing nor obtrusive. Yet, does have the acumen to bring waffling points to closure and tactfully shorten long-winded pontifications, if any. She has some wit and humor and unites the team in a feeling of togetherness. She works toward a consensus based upon legitimate discourse and the merits of the case. She is admired and respected by her team colleagues.

### TEAM TASKS LARGELY LEADER SPECIFIC

| | | |
|---|---|---|
| Chair Meetings | Insures Closure on Points | Secures Environment |
| Maintain Focus | Praises/Recognizes Members | Unites the Group |
| Schedule Meetings | Maintains Tempo | Prepares Agendas |
| Invite Ad-hoc Members | Communicates with Sponsor | Issues Reports |

## Team Sponsor

A team sponsor is a person of substantial authority or respect whose sanction gives life to a team. The team sponsor, just as a "walkathon" sponsor, is not necessarily the project originator or champion. The sponsor could well be the one that authorized resources for the team effort.

## Team Champion

Champion is the individual largely credited with driving the team mission and undertaking: often the team leader. The word champion is usually ascribed to someone who is plowing new ground: driving an innovative, controversial, or difficult assignment. Champion is a dynamic, energetic term usually earned for confronting a difficult challenge and coming out victorious. One would not use the term champion to describe the routine assembling of a team for ordinary purposes.

## Group Dynamics: Style and Structure

How a team operates can and usually is governed by the team leader's style.

The most democratic or egalitarian style figuratively takes the shape of a circle or closed loop of some recognizable shape.

The fan structure is or can be more tightly controlled and is useful when quicker results or very little two way conversation is involved. Usually the chair or leader exhibiting this style will sit at the end of the table, in the turkey carving position.

## Case Study: Library Team Fan Structure

I, along with a half dozen others, was solicited to sit on a library committee. Gathering for the initial meeting, we were greeted by the chair, a retired school teacher whom it was clear was in command. She sat in the lone chair on one wide side of the rectangular table; the remaining team members sat across from her on the opposite side. The physical shape resembled a fan with no doubt as to where the focal point would be.

Things did not go well, and the initial meeting was soon to be known as the final one.

At the time I faulted the chair, but in retrospect I now see it differently. In fairness, some of the team member's input was too grandiose and unnecessary for the task at hand. And what style would one expect from that grand lady who had stood in the front of the class in a similar fashion for forty some years? That style is what she knew. In a way she was a benevolent autocrat.

## Rescued But Died In The Process: Case in Point

Rescue is normally regarded as an act of mercy or a virtuous deed; the rescuer being labeled a prince or princess.

But not always so.

The management team in a charitable organization consisted of four employee staffers and five volunteer directors; the directors being prominent citizens in the community. This team formulated policy and made major decisions.

At issue one evening meeting was the alleged misconduct of one staffer in the handling of his crew. Feedback from workers and other supervisors alike was that this particular individual, call him Harry, was overbearing, zealous, and nearly brutal in dealing with employees.

This was the second time, following an earlier warning, that Harry was being reprimanded by the management team. The team exchanged robust dialogue with Harry, putting him on notice of the severity of his status as a permanent employee.

However, just when the message seemed to be sinking in a little, one member came to Harry's rescue with some favorable comments on his performance. At that intervention, another director chimed in with a patronizing litany of compliments about Harry which had him beaming. The rest of the team were soon silenced and that was that for the evening.

You might guess what happened. Armed with what Harry felt was a solid vote of confidence, he continued his abusive behavior, changing not one whit.

Harry was fired.

The rescuers, in retrospect, did him a disservice and contributed to his downfall by supporting his ill behavior; while others had sought to encourage him to change to acceptable norms.

Message to be learned from this story is that sometimes by meaning well, you can overdo it, and harm a person with your intended kindness. The role of rescuer is not a valid team function, assigned to a member, but rather a tactic to be used with discretion by all.

## TEAM DYNAMICS
## TABLE POSITIONS: IT MATTERS

The chair who sits at the end of the table – carves the turkey. Tends to create an authoritative image.

A round table promotes equality and eye contact.

Arena

A long, narrow table promotes mid-table participation, excluding end positions.

Best way to neutralize a fiery or hostile opponent; sit next to them.

# Ego States and the Team Process

An integral concept of Eric Berne's work in Transactional Analysis is the notion that people operate out of various ego states. An ego state in this circumstance being described as a set of internal feelings that result in a characteristic set of behavior patterns.

The model related to ego states forms the PAC model; an acronym for Parent, Adult, Child. A further refinement occurs in that the parent can be separated by behaviors described as either a critical or nurturing parent. Additionally, the child ego state can be expressed as either the fun child or the adaptive child.

None of the ego states are inherently good or bad in and of themselves; with possibly the adult state being the most consistent in behavior.

The basic assumption of the PAC model is that a person is, at anytime, in one of the three ego states. And, every person, in varying degrees, transacts in all the ego states, but not simultaneously.

I witnessed one quick reversal of the child ego states. A toddler waiting in a doctor's office, curiously crawled over to the closed door and pushed her fingers under the small opening at the bottom. A fun child behavior. Inside, a patient playfully grabbed the protruding fingers and squeezed them gently. The surprised child quickly retreated to her chair, and there remained for the balance of the wait; an adaptive child behavior.

Regarding the group dynamics which occur during a team process, a blend of behavioral styles and ego states will produce the best results.

| PAC MODEL ILLUSTRATED | | |
|---|---|---|
| **EGO STATES** | **DESCRIPTORS** | **CHARACTERISTICS** |
| **P** <br> PARENT | Nurturing Parent <br> Caring Nurturing <br> Rescuing | Interactions are soft spoken, sympathetic, understanding and comforting. |
| | Critical Parent <br> Controls Directs <br> Judges | Serious demeanor with emphasis on do's and don'ts, prejudicial. |
| **A** <br> ADULT | Task Oriented <br> Processes Data <br> Asks Questions <br> Provides Answers <br> Emotionally Detached | Calm, Cool, Collected Logic, reasoning, and problem solving. |
| **C** <br> CHILD | Fun Child <br> Curious Imaginative <br> Lively | Active, Animated, risk taker, unbridled, and adventuresome. |
| | Adaptive Child <br> Obedient Dependent <br> Guided | Conforms and compromises and seeks help |

Staying in the adult mode continually makes for a very sterile process; rich in logic but short perhaps on fun and celebration. A mixture of critical parent is also beneficial as a good dose will counteract the overly comfortable feeling encountered when Groupthink sets in.

The team process will normally follow a systematic work plan sequence; and, in fact perhaps a myriad of sub-topical work plans following largely the same sequence. One systematic approach being the Value Engineering job plan consisting of five phases: Information Gathering, Function Analysis, Idea Generation, Evaluation/Recommendation, and Implementation.

The lesson to be drawn from ego states concepts is that certain ego states are more appropriate in certain phases of team processes than others.

## Information Gathering – *Adult Ego State*

For example, the information gathering phase requires the logic and reasoning associated with the adult ego state. Accuracy, preciseness, and completeness of data is what is needed at this time. Information Gathering can be characterized as somewhat a mechanical process.

## Idea Generation Phase – *Fun Child*

However, when the team enters the Idea Generation or Brainstorming phase, then the imaginative fun child is what is called for. In this phase, the emphasis is on unbridled thought and free expression of possibilities. One critical feature here should be to defer judgment of proposals while they are yet being developed. As such, the critical parent ego state should take a long vacation at this point.

## Evaluating Ideas – *Parent/Adult*

Once all the ideas are in, then at some point comes the judicial process of evaluating ideas for soundness. This is a good time to perhaps unlock the door and let the parent in; both of them. The nurturing parent ego state can serve as an idea advocate; the critical parent ego state as the devil's advocate, possessor of the jaundiced eye.

Team processes and roles correspond to values held by team members which manifest in behaviors and actions. Illustrated is various team processes, tasks and roles which relate to the prevailing ego states generally associated with a particular behavior.

## GLITZY TECHNIQUES

Glitzy techniques used in team sessions by some creative advocates run the gamut from the ridiculous to the sublime; from permission meters, direction arrows, honking horns, and soup to nuts. As you might surmise, I do not favor heavy use of these. Some concepts that I have observed, but would not recommend doing often, follow.

## Lionel Train Wreck Ploy

One technique suggested to ward off excessive straying off the topic by a windy team member is the Lionel Train Wreck Ploy. A train engine is mounted on a circular track, featured as a centerpiece on the meeting room table. The concept being that when a team member "gets off the track," another member tips the train off the track as a signal.

## Powder Puff Ball Rebuff

To insure harmony within a team, powder puff balls are available to team members to hurl at an individual who seemingly is negative or at odds with the general consensus of the team.

## Gimmick Cards

Gimmick Cards are mini-cards carrying preconceived messages as a response to a fellow team member's position or negative reaction to a popularly held notion. Road-block tickets or cards are a common example of this concept. In lieu of saying the obvious to a fellow team member, these cards serve as a carrier of the unspoken word. For example, a negative response to a proposed idea might be greeted with a card stating, "defer judgment". Sometimes, this gimmick works well; and sometimes it back-fires. The card receiver might delight in accumulating cards or, Heaven forbid, the dealer might run out of cards.

Fun is fun, and I probably wouldn't have too much problem with techniques such as the tipped train or powder puff toss if they were spontaneous and short-lived. Contin-ued use lessens their effectiveness and probably ends up being a counter-productive tactic.

# RULES FOR TEAM BEHAVIOR IN MEETINGS:

With the growing number of organizations relying on multi-functional teams for major improvements, team rules are becoming more prominent. As sometimes happens with new concepts, the pendulum often swings too far, and subsequently moderates. In the following table, some of the more commonly developed rules are listed along with some relative comments.

# COMMENTS ON EXPRESSED TEAM RULES

| PROPOSED TEAM RULE: | POSITIVE REACTION: | CONCERNS: |
|---|---|---|
| 1. Mandatory meeting attendance | Solid attendance is prized prized | Some flexibility is needed. |
| 2. No hidden agendas | A given. | None. |
| 3. Leave feelings at the meeting | A given. | A reminder is sometimes necessary after a hard day. |
| 4. Respect others opinions | A given. | None. |
| 5. Regular schedule | Planned continuity. | Becomes an automatic routine. |
| 6. Have fun. | A plus. | Satisfaction might be more descriptive |
| 7. Covenant contracts | None. | If an informal contract is needed in an informal group, trouble looms |
| 8. There are no rules. | Like the wide open thrust. | Discretion necessary. |
| 9. Two minute talking rule. | Limits loquacious members. | Too limiting and childish. |
| 10. Self empowered. | Sounds good. | Sometimes mouthed, not backed. |
| 11. Two hour meeting maximum | Excellent for normal projects. | Match task with time. |
| 12. Absolute starting time. | Good, within reason. | Focus on form, not task. |
| 13. Formal agenda. | Excellent idea. | Not unless flexible. |
| 14. Substitute members | Mixed feelings-better than none. | Continuity and efficiency loss. |

# GOODIES AND BADDIES ABOUT TEAM FUNCTIONING:

| BADDIES: | GOODIES: |
|---|---|
| 1. Group not sized correctly | 5-7 regular members |

| Too small | Too large |
|---|---|
| 2 people | 10 people |

| BADDIES: | GOODIES: |
|---|---|
| 2. Not time driven | Attentive to target completion dates. |
| 3. Hostility among members | Harmony, respect and trust. |
| 4. Groupthink | Healthy difference and dialogue. |
| 5. Dominant verbal members | Egalitarian functioning. |
| 6. Uncertainty about objective or project scope | Well defined objective and desired outomce |
| 7. Lukewarm or compliance commitment only | A driving enthusiasm. |
| 8. Individuality lost | Team players, recognized for individual contribution as well. |
| 9. Team project requirements might jeopardize primary job position | Prime job scaled back if necessary in order to handle both requirements effectively |
| 10. Insufficient funds and resources to implement actions | Adequate funding controlled by team. |

# CHAPTER SEVEN
## COMMUNICATIONS IN TEAMS

Communication can be simply thought of as the process of creating common meaning and mutual understanding. One should take particular note of the precepts, common meaning, and mutual understanding. It is easy to blithely gloss over the precepts as given, but they are all important: particularly in team activities.

Illustration in point. A major manufacturer of underground mining equipment was facing shrinking profit margins on one of its major product lines. Fact was, manufacturing cost was moving uncomfortably close to market selling price. Given the existing market dynamics, increasing the product selling price was neither a popular nor a feasible option. Doing a Pareto cost analysis, it was soon leaned that raw steel comprised the largest single cost item. Therefore, if margins were to improve, some cost relief would have to be provided there.

A group, composed of reps from the steel supplier and various internal functional managers, met as a team to discuss ways to improve costs. As might be expected, traditional ideas were aired, such as: buy steel in larger tonnage, roll longer steel plate at the mill, jawbone for a more favorable price per pound, and so on. The two hour meeting didn't net much improvement and was subsequently in the process of being adjourned with participants standing, preparing to leave.

Then, a casual comment emerged from the company metallurgist that was soon to electrify the group. He said, rather dryly, "Well, we could save a lot of money, but we need the specified steel because of the sulfuric acid condition in mines which attack other metals." The steel supplier rep responded in an almost contentious tone, "No, the reason you are buying that particular steel is because of its strength characteristics." "Not so," the metallurgist persevered, "strength is not the issue: we are buying that particular steel for its outstanding corrosion resisting qualities, for which it is eminently known." To which the steel supplier explained, "It is true that the steel provides excellent corrosion resisting qualities; but, only in an external environment. It buys you nothing in a closed environment such as a mine. The nature of the steel is that it works through a series of alternating conditions such as rain, sun, hot, and cold wherein it keeps cleansing itself."

Immediately, the group sat down again. We were looking at a quarter-million dollar cost savings with a stroke of the pen and at no loss in customer value. The problem here came from mutual misunderstanding. Each party had an honest wrong belief. And, but for a casual comment at the right time, or perhaps a later Value Engineering study, the savings would not have occurred.

## VALUE MISMATCH PERCEPTIONS
## HONEST WRONG BELIEFS

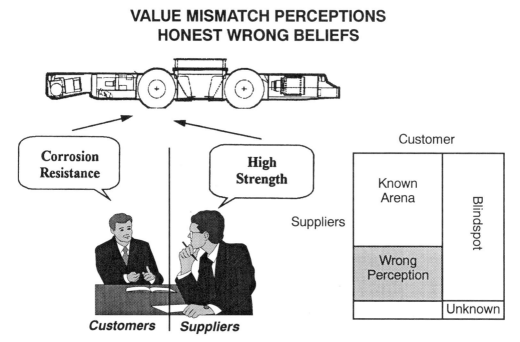

As mentioned earlier, mutual understanding is an important element in team processes. Everyone has seen examples of communication glitches, and one has to wonder why it happens if we are all speaking the same language. The answer lies in what is heard, in deference to what is spoken, and what is perceived by the listener versus what is intended by the speaker.

For example, look at some of the following from my memorabilia file:

- A letter arrived from Hawaii addressing me as "Commissar King": mistaking my request for hotel information for Thomas R. King. Who knows, the receptionist may have been a transplanted Russian.

- Another time, I errantly waited endlessly for a pizza pick-up as there was no pizza ready for Tom King. An hour later, the cashier found a cold pizza waiting for a pick-up by Mr. Tomkins.

- When my children were in high school in Franklin, PA, an away football game was being held with the Warren Dragons. The players bus went correctly to Warren, PA – the student body bus went instead to Warren, OH – each city of which was equal distance from Franklin. Obviously, not much cheering was heard for the Franklin Knights that evening.

- An important reference letter for a job seeker read, "I cannot recommend Mister X too highly." I always wondered whether the message was intended as glowing praise or a veiled hint of hidden truth to the contrary.

- Finally, looking for a way to warn local residents of the possibility of radioactive fallout from the Three-Mile Nuclear accident in south eastern PA, the town fathers rang the alarm sirens. Instead of people staying in their houses as was contemplated, people stormed outside to see what the problem was.

There are a variety of techniques to improve or insure conscious communication in team activities. Understanding and practicing them will help maintain adequate communication in the group dynamics process, so vital to a team's success.

## COMMUNICATION MODELS: The Johari Window Concept

The Johari Window is an excellent way to visually highlight the communication flow needed in team activities. The name Johari Window is derived from the window-like matrix that highlights the concept, Johari, from the shortened first names of Joseph Luft and Harry Ingram.

The Johari Window Concept is based on the notion that, in communications between individuals, or among team participants, there is information that is known, and other information that is unknown, at least to some of the participants. This is illustrated in the figure below.

### JOHARI WINDOW
#### Information that:

|  | I Know | I Didn't Know |
|---|---|---|
| You Know | I<br>Arena | II<br>Blind Spot |
| You Didn't Know | III<br>Facade | IV<br>Unknown |

The Johari window blocks are labeled by the following terms:

## Arena
The common area of understanding by all, essentially, the working arena.

## Unknown
That area which represents perhaps the undiscovered or germane points related to the subject that are not yet known.

## Blind Spot
Information on the topic or subject that is known by others involved, but not yet known to yourself.

## Facade
Information which I, as a participant, would know that others don't, and is yet unrevealed to them.

In effective two-way communications, each party seeks to enlarge the arena. This is done through "my disclosures and your feedback." The use of multi-functional teams to enlarge the arena on difficult projects is a natural and widely used concept.

At the same time, the arena is enlarged, the blind spot and the facade is being shrunk.

The unknown block in the window is then open to investigation and discovery which, if successfully done, will shrink that area. See illustration.

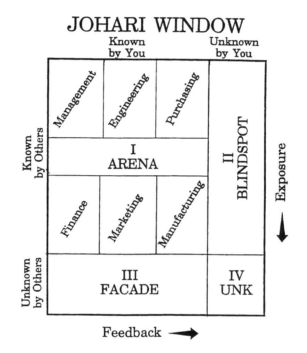

Team concept utilizing members from
multi-functional areas will increase the working arena.

## WHAT HOLDS PEOPLE BACK FROM SPEAKING UP IN A GROUP?

Team members are selected on the basis that they have something important to contribute to the task being addressed. It is not necessary for each member to vocalize or contribute evenly in the process. Each will have a different set of skills, experiences, and insight to bring to bear on the issues being considered.

However, individuals on certain efforts will not participate in an active manner within their capability; or having participated earlier in the group dynamics process may now be withholding their services. Why? The following table lists probable causes for this dormant behavior and what remedies an effective facilitator, whether a team leader or fellow colleague, can do about it.

**SYMPTOM:** Members not participating well or speaking up in a group or team meeting.

| POTENTIAL CAUSE | REMEDY |
|---|---|
| A. Shyness or timidity | Directly invite their input. Occasionally request team members to put their thoughts in writing. |
| B. Feeling discounted due to a prior putdown | An ounce of prevention is worth a pound of cure here. Set the standard practice up front of deferring judgement. |
| C. Intimidated by immediate supervisors also being in the same group, team, or meeting. | Assess up-front in team member selection if supervisor/subordinate cast on same team is appropriate. |
| D. Fear of embarrassment due to a question sounding dumb. | Establish an atmosphere of wide open, creative thinking – anything goes. |
| E. Can't get a word in edgewise. | Limit size of group to only that which is absolutely necessary. Consider forming sub-teams or adding ad-hoc members when greater input is needed. Tactfully shorten input from verbose members. |
| F. Member doesn't really agree, understand or have commitment to the project scope. | Re-examine project for validity. Discuss privately with member or discuss openly with group in an adult, candid manner. |
| G. Project not withn member's capability or ability to influence. | Mutually agree to withdraw member from project as a mismatch. |
| H. Mind and thoughts are preoccupied with personal problems. | Show patience and caring. Be helpful and compassionate if within your ability to alleviate the situation. Consider a leave of absence from team participation. |

# Dutiful Listening

Efficiency is not the same as effectiveness. Some have characterized efficiency as doing a job right; effectiveness, doing the right job. I would enlarge the simplified definition of effectiveness to include the degree to which outcomes satisfy expectations. In that regard, efficiency must be considered a how to, and in a sense, a collateral issue.

There has been an enormous amount of effort directed toward improving the efficiency of team dynamics. Ground rules for team membership behavior is one issue.

Suggestions range from mandatory attendance, five minute talking rule, to catered donuts and covenants.

Some are good; but in actuality, function is more important than form. Output or achievement is all important.

I would like to highlight a technique for facilitators that often enhances effectiveness; however, flies in the face of efficiency.

The technique is called dutiful listening.

Let me illustrate.

Picture yourself observing a team meeting through a one-way mirror. The chair is definitely in charge. She pounds the gavel at eight o'clock sharp. Minutes from the last meeting are read, seconded and approved. Susan, laughingly, begins to relay a funny happening in her neighborhood that occurred the evening before. The chair cuts Susan off in near mid-sentence, with a polite but noticeable admonishment; "Let's talk about that later; we now must address the task at hand". And the chair further shows acumen in leading efficient group activities. Sitting at the end of the table, in the turkey carving position, she asks each in turn what each member of the team thinks about a particular issue. She orchestrates the team as a first grade teacher might in sounding out the ABC's. It is an orderly process indeed. During a subsequent quest for ideas, the group is instructed to throw foam balls at a member who had the temerity to question a proposal that was laid on the table. No negotiation allowed here.

Tough Tracy they nicknamed her. What a team leader! To the casual observer, a first look might seem that this was a well ordered, well run meeting. Old Bosso, a theory X type puffing on an oversized cigar, would beam with pride at his protégé passing it on down.

The problem is with IT.

The reality of all this is that people are people – not cattle. Conversely, observe through another window a team that currently seems to be laboring. Harry is expanding the merits of an idea proposed with the same rigor as a liege defending his inheritance.

Harry is the longest, continual standing member of an idea review team in a continuous improvement program; having served on the same functional team for two decades. Why that long? Why not have vital fresh blood in the position.

The reality is that Harry is vital. He knows the product. He knows and understands the people. He is an agent for change. Harry has staying power. He is an invaluable resource. His shortcoming is that in communicating thoughts and ideas, especially good ones, he beats the issue to death; detail after detail in getting the point across. Team members find themselves helping Harry finish his dialogue to speed things up. Sometimes team members chime in, almost in total surrender "I'll do it". Enough, I'm convinced, to which Harry will add more verbiage in overkill, long after making his sell.

It really takes the patience of Job, a biblical comparison here, to listen to Harry's droning on.

But, it pays off.

I call the virtue – dutiful listening. Not necessarily patient listening but a dutiful obligation of sorts. It is a small price to pay for the very excellent and dedicated performance Harry, the senior member provides to the team. No one doubts his dedication. No one questions his expertise.

He has been the glue of this committee team over the years; the one who challenged reluctant engineers and production workers alike to objectively implement change.

Certainly the prospect of inviting Harry to attend communication and interpersonal skill training is contemplated; and this occurred.

Not much lasting change occurred.

Yet when you look at the situation in an evaluation sense, did we really want to change Harry all that much.

The fear of loss certainly seemed to override the promise of gain if we changed his modus operandi by emphasizing his shortcomings.

Which of course paled in comparison to his contributions.

## PERCEPTIONS & REALITY

There is a classic story told of a leader who had messengers put to death whenever he didn't like the message. Thereafter, he did not receive many messages he didn't like. In present day organizations, nothing this drastic occurs. Nevertheless, it does happen in a lesser fashion when a manager of autocratic bent refuses to face up to unpopular news, about which little or nothing can be done.

I'm reminded of a circumstance that occurred some years ago. I was visiting a company which was nearing a vote on an organizing effort. The general manager had started the company and had indeed put his heart and soul into it. It was now owned by others, with him staying on as the top manager. On one occasion, when times were tough, he generously (with risk) drew on his own personal check to cover the payroll. As I sat with him, he polled his team of supervisors one by one in an oral straw vote to see how the organizing effort might be leaning. One after another, they played the song he wanted to hear:

"Mr. Jones, I'm thinking that all ten of my men will vote 'No'."
"Mr. Jones, I believe twelve will vote 'No' , one 'Yes", and the other uncertain."

And on it went through other supervisors with similar responses. He slapped me on the knee, smiled, and basked in preliminary victory. About a week later, back home, I called my friend on another matter, but casually asked about the organizing vote. Following a brief silence, he relayed the news: something on the order of one hundred fifty favoring the union, ten or so opposed. A stunning reversal.

I could only conclude that his subordinates were telling him what they knew he desired to hear. What I could not be sure of is whether they delivered him pleasant news out of fear or out of compassion for his feelings. Not for a minute do I think the supervisors could have misread their employees intentions that badly.

The moral of this happening, if there is one, is that an atmosphere of open communication and respectful candor must exist among team players and managers must be willing to hear it.

# CHAPTER EIGHT
## GROUPTHINK

## EVERYONE PULLING IN THE SAME DIRECTION:
## Not Necessarily a Good Idea

All members of a team or group pulling in the same direction is not a good idea if they are all headed lockstep in the wrong direction. For example, it should not have been a mutinous matter if a brazen lieutenant in General Custer's command had uttered skepticism at Custer's fateful strategies. And, if only a few individuals in Jim Jones' following had stiffened their backbone, perhaps two hundred or so victims wouldn't have swallowed poison marching to their deaths.

While it is true that business teams don't operate in such an extraordinary manner; nevertheless, they have their foolish moments. One management team in a major corporation on the outskirts of Pittsburgh was found to have implemented a scheme to beat workers out of expected benefits. The trick was to keep a computerized list of employees as they approached the vesting phase, then dump individuals off the roster. They even had a disguised acronym code name to describe the program that was held incognito.

*Mutual trust?* it's an age old story, "One is always strong enough to bear up under another's grief."

## GROUPTHINK:
## A Condition Detracting from Team Performance

Among teams, Groupthink as we know it, is not a favorable condition. The concept for Groupthink has, at its roots, the conformity pressures that a team exerts, consciously or unconsciously, in order to assure group cohesiveness and harmony. It is natural for team members to want to maintain the integrity of a group. Seldom do members want to appear as mavericks or a lone dissenting voice in the face of a majority. In the extreme condition, there is such a strong tendency to agree that one is loathe to speak up with a personal concern.

Groupthink is not a rare phenomenon. It happens in personal situations with regularity in groups much less formal than a team. For example:

- A phone call is received from Sister Sarah whom you have not seen for some time. She requests your participation in pitching in five hundred dollars in lieu of your normal gift to stepparents, to send them to Turkey. She adds that she has contacted your other siblings who are warm to the idea.

Dilemma? You might or might not want to say yes. For one thing, you are wondering why this new found religion finally seized Sarah; and, is a trip to Turkey really appropriate. Your gut tells you to decline; but, here you sit, the most well to do of your siblings. Do you cave in in order to appear just as gracious?

- A group of orderlies is having lunch and casual chatter together when one good Samaritan gets a bright idea. "Five dollars doesn't go far these days, guys. Let's all throw in twenty-five dollars each toward the custodian's appreciation gift this year. We can all afford it."

One suddenly wishes the twenty minute lunch period had been fifteen minutes instead. While some colleagues, although looking puzzled, slowly nod approval, you contemplate the process. You are pondering why magnanimous Gertie, the suggester, previously declined union membership because of the outrageous dues – had short arms and deep pockets during the United Way fund drive – now dumps this overkill on the group. You are reluctant to look like a cheapskate for twenty bucks or so. What do you do?

While these anecdotes are colored just a shade, they are drawn from actual experiences in everyday life. Symptoms of Groupthink appear in business organizations far more often than they do in ordinary life. One sure combination for developing Groupthink within a team is having an egotistical superior on the same team as subordinates. Very quickly, the scenarios become the likes of the now concluded Johnny Carson television talk show. Johnny, speaking pearls of wisdom while attentive and patronizing Ed McMann, responds with hearty laughter and a big, cheery, "You are correct, sir!" The same type of dutiful following happens in teams or group settings, giving a powerful boss with powerful, albeit, ill conceived convictions. The outcome is predictable. Feigned agreement or silence by subordinates up front, but commensurate damaging dialogue behind the walls.

To some extent, everyone knows what reality is. You can change a person's behavior without changing his or her perception. Dr. Irving L. Janus is credited with doing much to unravel the mysteries of Groupthink. He was instrumental in developing ideas on how to prevent its unwanted occurrence and how to deal with it once it has occurred.

# SYMPTOMS AND MANIFESTATIONS OF GROUPTHINK

## 1. Illusions of Unanimity

Members avoid challenging a popular view on what appears to be a majority opinion.

## 2. Silence of Team Members

Means consent or agreement with the issues or proposals.

## 3. Internal Pressure

Just as a border collie dog brings straying sheep back into the herd, so may the internal pressure of a team be applied to ring in a dissenting member.

## 3. Rationalization

Rationalization may occur as a collective group phenomenon to explain away an issue that should be given serious attention. Rationalization can also be restricted to a single member who, rather than confront the team with unfavorable news, neutralizes his true thoughts.

## 4. Adversarial Discounting

Groupthink is taking over whenever those holding opposing views are routinely held as non-consequential or incompetent by the group majority.

Adapted from *Groupthink,* Dr. I.L. Janis

# COUNTERACTING THE GROUPTHINK PHENOMENON

Six tactics to avoid falling prey to the groupthink phenomenon follow:

1. Team should be composed of members having various backgrounds.

2. Initially, idea generation should take priority: deferring judgment until later.

3. Team leader should encourage a diversity of viewpoints.

4. Recognize that candor and disagreement on issues can be as legitimate as loyalty and agreement.

5. Devil's advocate positions in team processes should be tolerated.

6. Bounce proposed idea solutions off of people external to the team.

# CHAPTER NINE
## TEAM DECISION MAKING

Decision making in teams is best derived through consensus by dialogue rather than by voting on majority rule.

Consensus comes through a reasoning process that makes use of evaluation and risk analysis techniques when necessary, along with weight given to various arguments.

Positioning, persuasion, and posturing by team members toward a particular outcome is normal in open organizations. In order to maintain team harmony and effect good decisions, knowledge of available techniques and appropriate interpersonal skills loom large in a team member's skills bag.

---

### TEAM DECISION MAKING
### BY TYPE

1. Settlement by consensus

2. Mechanical
   Decision by the majority
   Let the numbers read
   Voting

3. Compromise
   Members surrender something they value in trade for an
   outcome they can support.

4. Domination
   Win-lose
   One-sided gains at the distress of the other

---

# Technically Sound Decisions Don't Always Win

If you ever need convincing that solutions of the highest technical quality don't always get implemented, or quickly, here are two classics to consider: metric system and the keyboard layout.

The metric issue is well known: metric being pretty much a system of tens, while the more romantic imperial system consists of rods, furlongs, and the king's foot. The changeover to metric has been slow in coming, but it now appears that only two countries remain on the imperial system of measurement.

The keyboard issue on typewriters and computers is a strange situation. Everyone from Junior to Grandmother is familiar with the "QWERTY" top line layout on keyboard. Logic would suggest that the reason for this arrangement was to improve operator efficiency. That is, the keys would be arranged systematically to take advantage of alphabet letters that were most commonly used together. The fact is that the letters were arranged that way in 1867 by typewriter inventor Christopher Sholes to slow the typist down. That's the incredible truth.

In early typewriter design, the keys fell mechanically back by gravity. Consequently, if struck too fast, they would jam. Since then, gravity is no longer a design factor, and there exists two little known keyboards that can be utilized about twenty-five percent faster. One is the DVORAK keyboard named after its inventor, Professor Dvorak.

Yet, this good technical solution seems destined for the field of broken dreams except for some persisting advocates. Reasons include standardization, learning curves, and resistance to change: bearing out the fact that acceptance by decision makers can override technically superior solutions.

**The DVORAK keyboard, as illustrated, is thought to improve typing efficiency about 25% over the traditional design.**
**Courtesy: Dvorak International**

## Consensus Team Decisions

There are two aspects of gaining consensus regarding team decisions. The first is finding agreement within the team: the other being acceptance by ultimate decision makers outside the team. If the team who labored extensively on the task cannot reach consensus, there is little expectation that others will view the team's findings as conclusive.

Rarely in organization settings is there but one solution to a task or problem. Most always there is an array of alternatives, some perceived as being various degrees of magnitude better than others with team members differing in opinion. Consensus must therefore be reached through the mediating power of logic, facts, influence, and persuasion.

Persuasion is thought to begin by gaining and maintaining the other's attention. In communication exchanges, the first few minutes of dialogue are extremely important and can be called an interest threshold. This threshold must be crossed early if the individual you are trying to influence is to remain alert and receptive. Attention, once lost, is difficult to retain because the continuity of thought has been interrupted. Some principles which work well towards team consensus:

- Listen and comprehend. Perhaps other team members have valid points that should be given greater weight in the decision process.

- Focus on key issues without interjecting trifles or extraneous data.

- Stay calm: avoid over-reaction.

- Don't name drop or be too greatly affected by the dropped name of a third party. The job is the boss. If a person continually drops names, it's a pretty good sign their own argument is weak.

- Compromise on small issues that mean little.

- Every member must have their status. Just as you would not corner a wounded bear in a cave, team members should not be backed into a corner with no escape route. If this occurs, you will certainly win the battle: it is equally certain that you will lose the war.

## Insider Status

There are ways to hedge your bet in getting approval externally for the team's recommendations. Keeping the eventual decision makers appraised of the team's progress at certain milestones is one tactic. Remember that power figures such as decision makers do not relish major surprises: sometimes not even favorable ones as they might feel upstaged. They want to know what's going down.

One ingredient for success is insuring that decision makers will have had a hand in the team project as it progressed. That involvement can occur in various subtle ways. One of the most effective is for the decision maker to have had a respected subordinate, or choice appointee, on the team as an official member. His or her interests will be represented. He will  have what I call - **Insider Status.**

Lets examine a case study where an autonomous team worked on a project in a product manager's turf area without input from that functional area.

Seeking to improve customer value, a Value Engineering group consisting of four individuals was organized as a function reporting to the general manager. Anxious to ply their trade of value fundamentals they had recently learned in an outside seminar, they selected a current product offering.

Rather than invite team members from other functions in a matrix role, they went it alone. It seems they wanted to establish their credibility as a viable function and chose this manner in which to proceed. Cloistered in their own arena, the value team proceeded to develop ideas to improve value on a popular product line.

The team came up with a myriad of potential improvements affecting the design, manufacture, and procurement of various components: some very good ones, and some perhaps not so good. After three months of virtually secret activity, they produced a final report with copious amounts of recommendations and documentation. This they presented to the staff at a formal meeting, along with glossy pictures and bio's of themselves as project architects. End result? The design engineer responsible for the product line eventually stonewalled the study and dismissed their findings as fruitless, uninvited and unworthy.

The project died and, along with it, the value team's dream. It doesn't take a genius to figure out what happened.

The decision maker had no insider status into the happenings of the team effort as it progressed. He was slighted, embarrassed. Sometimes the presence of even a junior participant from a decision maker's area will be sufficient to sustain or garner the needed confidence and to avoid a slight and a perceived discount of sensitivities involved.

# EVALUATION TECHNIQUES

Several good techniques exist for evaluating the worth of an idea or proposed solution to a problem. Some of these are:

1. Individual Assessment
2. Team Consensus
3. Combinex
4. Matrix Analysis
5. PET-Project Evaluation Technique
6. Risk Analysis

## Individual Assessment

This method is not as imprecise as it would first appear, and is based primarily on factors, such as:

- Experience
- Comparisons
- Judgment
- Knowledge
- Intuition

People buy, sell, and trade in their daily life and ultimately develop a sense for the worth of goods, functions, and services. Some, obviously, are more skilled at it than others.

Individual estimates play a vital role in even the more scientific approaches toward measuring worth.

## Team Consensus

Experience with several controlled group ranking exercises in university and industrial settings has convinced the author that teams ordinarily do better than individuals acting alone, in determining worth.

Group discussions, and the different input and skill levels brought by individuals to group activity, tend to counteract the extreme levels of bias and lack of information held by individuals on certain issues.

## Special Evaluation Techniques

Several good techniques exist for determining worth a little more scientifically. Most of these evolve around a matrix grid featuring paired comparisons.

- Numerical Evaluation
- Combinex Method
- Risk Analysis

## POSITIONING

Positioning by team members on important issues is a legitimate activity if done for the right reasons. It is not unusual for individual team members to come to meetings with strong opinions on particularly contentious points and some are well supported by logic – others perhaps by emotion. Convincing becomes an art, particularly when fellow team members may be in disagreement. One cardinal rule in situations such as this, is: "listen more than you talk."

Be open – maybe the other person really has something. What the team is looking for is consensus, not necessarily one hundred percent agreement. But, an outcome that can be supported by all. As a tactic, it is not treasonous to seek out another team member separate from the meeting in order to bounce your thoughts and feelings off of them. Your logic might make a lot of sense. And, too, the other colleague might modify or add to your conclusions to make the concept more palatable.

This relationship with another member is termed a "pairing" of sorts. Also the benefit of one on one dialogues might unconsciously lead to a beneficial symbiotic relationship that manifests favorably at team meetings. Clock time with another individual invariably builds trust, providing, of course, there exists no trace of politics or scheming towards a fellow team member.

Going into a meeting paired with another who both understands your position and agrees with it exponentially increases your chances of a wanted outcome.

## Argument to Convince

A jury decision is a classic example of the argument to convince within a group. In a jury situation, an initial straw vote to sound out the feelings of the group often finds them lopsided in their evaluation. Consequently, those holding the majority position will attempt to persuade the remaining members to change their point of view and gain consensus for a decision. If no consensus is reached early, the atmosphere will escalate into steadily increasing intensity, pressure, and uncomfortable feelings. The argument, if carried to the wall, goes through four phases.

The first phase is quite congenial: information is exchanged and viewpoints aired. At this juncture, if the minority concede, they will still be highly regarded and seen as solid team colleagues. In fact, their status might be elevated somewhat in that, to their credit, they proved open minded and able to reason. If unconvinced, the argument to convince moves up a notch.

In phase two, the intensity increases. The argument to convince takes on a gentle, but very noticeable prodding. If this extra measure works in winning the minority position over, all is forgiven. As a rule, the dissenting members will still enjoy legitimate status on the team and, in fact, may be highly respected for their tenacity.

If no consensus is reached at this point, phase three involves the attack. Dialogue gets very personal and one's lineage might take a verbal tongue lashing. The dispute is real, pressure is applied, and this increased diatribe will either cause the weak to capitulate or increase their determination to stay the course. Either way, following the attack, the dissenting members will become persona non grata, as true and equal members on the team.

The final phase results in complete polarization and the realization that no consensus will be reached. The collaboration ends. In the case of a trial, the result is a hung jury. Business teams go through much the same scenario in evaluating ideas or proposals when they are a house divided. It is interesting to note that, in the argument to convince, the sequence never changes: only the rate at which it occurs.

| ARGUMENT TO CONVINCE | | | |
|---|---|---|---|
| **Phase 1**<br>**Inform/Appeal** | **Phase 2**<br>**Prod** | **Phase 3**<br>**Attack** | **Phase 4**<br>**Sever** |

## NEGOTIATION TACTICS FOR TEAMS

A cardinal rule in negotiations is to never pass up the opportunity to keep your mouth shut. Therefore, by conscious effort, you can be a good listener and benefit your knowledge more by listening than talking.

In this respect, the concept of openness might be at odds with the spirit of the Johari Window concept.

In cooperative team efforts, it is ideal to keep the arena large and facade small; however, as a hard nose negotiating strategy, another tactic is often used. Disclose little; but ask pointed questions that will secure your needed information.

Six key points in team negotiation strategy follow:

1. Pre-planning is an important element in negotiation strategy. Objectives and

outcomes that are desired from the negotiating process should be well defined and understood by all members of the bargaining team. An agenda should exist to maintain focus during the process.

2. Your negotiation team should have a leader, or spokesperson, who will quarterback the team negotiation process.

3. Negotiate on home turf or familiar ground when possible. There is a psychological advantage to negotiating at the home quarters, especially when your position is strong.

4. Pass over difficult items; return to them later. Tough issues erode the momentum and enthusiasm.

5. Patience. The best anglers are those who sit quietly and wait after casting their bait in a prominent water. Call it patience. The same trait is true of a good negotiator. With patience, you can be a major force at the negotiating table and get more of what you want.

6. Negotiate with character. Practicing the Golden Rule cannot be faulted. Those who practice the opposite adage "Do others before they do you," don't do for very long.

## ROADBLOCKS

Roadblock is a term describing a decision and statement made without due consideration or logic. Generally, it is an automatic or conditioned negative response geared to prevent implementation of an idea. The resistance is nearly always in the form of a generality, rather an a specific. Further, it usually follows very quickly in the presentation of the idea.

### Typical Roadblocks

- That is not an original idea. It's been suggested before and didn't pan out.
- It's too much trouble to change and my department is up to it's ears in work.
- I don't like it and no one else will either.
- The product is doing all right and we don't want to risk anything new at this time.

Dealing with roadblocks requires good skills; particularly if you are interacting with supervisors. First point of business is to look inward and determine whether the resistance is really a roadblock. Perhaps the resistance is due to known facts in hand, and not just a pithy conditioned response.

For example, if your child wanted to go skating on an ice pond where the ice thickness was questionable, your negative response would hardly be frivolous. It would be an absolute correct one based on conscious thought.

The following situations are roadblocks; how might you address them?

ROADBLOCK NO. 1
"That proposal would cost a fortune to implement!"

ONE ANSWER

"Possibly you're right, but let's determine just how much and make a decision on that basis".

ROADBLOCK NO. 2

"Why change, we haven't had a failure on that part for 25 years".

ONE ANSWER

"That might be the clue that the safety factor is more than sufficient. Incidentally, have you taken a close look at the gross margin on your product lately. This change would help".

One tactic that is appropriate on some ideas that might be marginal is to ask for a test or trial; not necessarily a permanent change. It's difficult to refuse a trial, particularly if the test is controlled and the payoff, a handsome one.

Also, should the trial fail, old bosso is spared the embarrassment of having formally approved the idea; after all it was only a test, and could have gone either way.

---

## DOZEN IDEA HANDLING TIPS

- Treat each idea and idea submitter with respect.

- Contacting the idea originator is important.

- You are answering for an organization of which you and the idea originator are family.

- Keep responses brief – do not overwhelm the reader.

- Avoid cold, impersonal, obtrusive, and power tones.

- Do not use the words "reject" or "rejection".

- Do not use telegram type, choppy answers: use normal dialogue.

- Avoid "I" in answers – use "We"

- "Not original" is much less preferable than saying – "Has been considered previously."

- A good, polite, accurate answer reduces problems later.

- Provide answers that you would consider reasonable.

---

# CHAPTER TEN
## STAGNATING TEAMS: AND WHAT TO DO ABOUT THEM

All of us that have been involved with teams over the years find ourselves on a team that is going nowhere and taking us with them.

No one is more aware that a team is stagnating than the team members themselves. The bellwether signals are all too apparent: spirits are at a low ebb and the leader is about to declare victory and disband. Nevertheless, assuming the objective for which the team was originated is still valid, some different mode of operation may still salvage the effort. Let's look at some bellwether signs that the effort is sinking toward a fateful end.

---

### BELLWETHER SIGNS THAT THE TEAM IS IN TROUBLE

✗ Lately, meetings have been aborted and have become infrequent.

✗ Team member attendance has dropped off with some members partially attending, arriving later and/or leaving early.

✗ There exists this aura surrounding the team processing that is totally absent of humor. Team going through the motions.

✗ Team members may have left the team and assigned their spot to a subordinate.

✗ Copious meeting minutes that were circulated early in the team's life together now are skimpy, often neglected entirely.

✗ One team member candidly adds, "We stink, don't we?"

### YOU KNOW YOUR TEAM IS ABOUT TO DIE WHEN...

✓ Everyone leaves the meetings when the donuts are gone.

✓ A team member dials for Dr. Kevorkian.

✓ A member who used to whistle Bridge On the River Kwai now hums Taps.

---

Assuming it was a well perceived objective to begin with, understood by all, and the right players on the team, then the problem undoubtedly lies in the team process. Something is lacking and needs to change.

One common cause would be that the effort took so long in development that enthusiasm waned while key resources were consumed. The team was drained with no accomplishment to show.

In reflecting on the team's situation, they are probably at the low end of the conceptual Menninger Morale Curve. Developed by Karl Menninger, the concept can be adapted to a variety of applications, team progress being one. Mr. Menninger speaks of the Four Key Crises in beginning a new effort, such as the team project and its continuing life together.

- The *First Crisis* is the entrance, getting started, overcoming the inertia law of rest, and dealing with apprehension teams might have up front in the going.

- The *Second Crisis* occurs based on false expectations that the project will go smoothly and systematically toward a given outcome. But, harsh reality sets in. Obstacles are in the way and realities begin surfacing that this project is no "easy picking." It is complex, in some ways quite abstract, and concrete data hard to come by. Team members become a little puzzled.

- The *Third Crisis* is on the continuum where the stagnating team finds itself today. Frustration and acknowledgement of the dilemma is common knowledge. Should the team throw in the towel and chalk this one up to experience; or, to save face, should they dawdle along hoping for some serendipitous happening? It is a real crisis indeed at this point. The team will either find a way to turn this situation around and go on to success, or they will soon sink, fading into oblivion as a failed team.

- The *Fourth Crisis,* if not averted by a favorable turnabout, is separation and discontinuation of the team.

What to do about it? How to turn this mess around? Turnarounds are not easy.

One of the first things the team needs to do is to acknowledge among itself the low level of operation it now has and the need for change.

Secondly, the team needs to focus forward rather than looking at past happenings with a jaundiced eye. You need ideas to move on, not justification for blame.

Thirdly, although not an absolute, it would be a good practice at this point to bring a trusted facilitator into the team bowels for a one day off-site meeting. This would be a time for renewal and refocusing on the stalemated issues.

Fourth, it is obvious the team needs energized. Energy is there, it is just hibernating for the moment. Two techniques might be the antidote here for turning the Menninger Morale Curve upward and back on track towards success. Try some fun. Revisit the task issues identified earlier with a free wheeling idea generating session. Brainstorming is one technique; but, expose the team to at least two other techniques as well.

Fifth, introduce a couple of systematic problem solving approaches that the team can become familiar with and use as the project moves forward. Given the situation, any of several techniques, all having a systematic approach, could be helpful. Among them:

- Value Engineering Job Plan
- Conventional Problem Solving Approach
- Force Field Analysis

Sixth, go for a quick win, even on small items. Momentum is needed, and quickly. Even small wins will recharge the team, regain some lost confidence, raise esteem, and provide inertia for continuing. Publish the positive happenings and celebrate a little.

Seventh, as meetings continue, the team may want to consider inviting Ad Hoc members to address special areas where expertise does not necessarily reside among team members.

## What Prevents Teams From Performing to High Levels of Efficiency & Skill?

In the case of the Pittsburgh Pirates baseball team in the mid-nineties, a major mystery it is not. Competing with major markets such as New York City and LA, whose resources seemed unlimited, the Pirates lost many players through free agency – unable to pay the high salaries players are commanding.

Different issues plague business teams from living up to expectations. Some major recurring contributors to shortfall performance were identified and rated by numerical evaluation techniques according to incidence.

Competing priorities caused teams the most trouble. In order of difficulty, the detractors were:

1. Competing priorities
2. Questionable commitment
3. Lack of authority
4. Time constraint
5. Wrong players
6. Key functions missing
7. Team incompatibility
8. Insufficient funding.

A review of the numerical evaluation matrix details the findings.

# NUMERICAL EVALUATION

What prevents teams from performing to high levels of efficiency and skill?

NUMERICAL EVALUATION IS A TECHNIQUE FOR MAKING PAIRED COMPARISONS OF TWO OR MORE ITEMS.

| ITEM | ITEMS BEING COMPARED | WEIGHT | RANK |
|------|----------------------|--------|------|
| A | Time constraints | 6 | 4 |
| B | Competing priorities | 13 | 1 |
| C | Lack authority | 9 | 3 |
| D | Wrong players | 6 | 5 |
| E | Key functions missing | 3 | 6 |
| F | Commitment questionable | 12 | 2 |
| G | Insufficient funding | 0 | 8 |
| H | Team incompatibility | 1 | 7 |

|   | B | C | D | E | F | G | H | I | J | K |
|---|---|---|---|---|---|---|---|---|---|---|
| A | B-1 | A-1 | A-1 | A-1 | F-2 | A-1 | A-2 |   |   |   |
|   | B | B-1 | B-2 | B-3 | B-1 | B-2 | B-3 |   |   |   |
|   |   | C | C-1 | C-2 | C-1 | C-3 | C-2 |   |   |   |
|   |   |   | D | D-2 | F-2 | D-2 | D-2 |   |   |   |
|   |   |   |   | E | F-2 | E-2 | E-1 |   |   |   |
|   |   |   |   |   | F | F-3 | F-3 |   |   |   |
|   |   |   |   |   |   | G | H-1 |   |   |   |
|   |   |   |   |   |   |   | H | I |   |   |

EVALUATION WEIGHT FACTORS

1. MINOR DIFFERENCE IN IMPORTANCE
2. MEDIUM DIFFERENCE IN IMPORTANCE
3. MAJOR DIFFERENCE IN IMPORTANCE

INSTRUCTIONS:
STEP 1: LIST THE ITEMS TO BE COMPARED
STEP 2: ONE AT A TIME, USING THE MATRIX TO GUIDE . . . COMPARE ITEMS AGAINST EACH OTHER USING A WEIGHT DIFFERENTIAL; A1, C2, ETC. (LETTER WOULD INDICATE WHICH ITEM WAS MORE IMPORTANT; THE NUMBER WOULD INDICATE THE DEGREE).
STEP 3: ADD THE NUMERICAL WEIGHTS FOR EACH ITEM
STEP 4: RANK IN IMPORTANCE BY NUMBER OF POINTS GATHERED

# GROUP DYNAMICS OF NON-PRODUCING TEAMS

Functional purposes of having teams is to get things done that are normally beyond the ordinary resources available to an individual at a given time. *Many hands make light the load* is a truism that leaves little room for argument. Yet, even with a reasonable selection of ordinarily capable team members, the effort often flutters and fails. Why? More importantly, what can we do about it? One initial step in formulating the ingredients for effective teams is to understand what it is that renders fruitless team efforts.

Some recurring team failures are inextricably linked to a particular constraint or operating mode. Certain of these I have labeled with pet names, highlighting their particular weakness, being:

- Squirrel Teams
- Nomad Teams
- Powerless Teams
- Slave Teams
- Mechanical Teams
- Plastic Teams

The important thing to consider is that one fatal flaw can be enough to sink a team's effort. Just as one small hole left unplugged can sink a canoe, one flaw may well be sufficient to render a team unproductive and barren.

Some attributes of the various non-productive team efforts follow:

## Squirrel Teams

Squirrel team members delight in accumulating data and mountains of paper. Their mode of operation is an incessant desire to demonstrate progress by the weight of the documentation accumulated. More is better. Meeting minutes and progress reports abound. As one U.S. Senator put it sixty years ago, "We'll explore and explore, only that and nothing more." The problem is – nothing productive happens. Completeness is often a virtue. However, when the collection of data, and paperwork in particular, is carried to extremes, the effort collapses under its own weight. One does not know where to start sorting through the fuzzy mess.

Largely, the teams reluctance to move forward is overt; however, other times it is covert. Overt is mere ineptness. Covert attitudes surface in downsizing efforts such as reengineering initiatives where the outcome might be unpleasant for team members as well.

## Nomad Teams

Nomad teams move about not certain where they are going or when they will arrive. They have not been given a clear objective nor a concrete sense of what they are really to be doing. They wander aimlessly.

Nomads usually get into this predicament being assigned by a steering committee to do an ill-defined thing: neither party of which knows what it is, exactly. Periodic progress reports are made – firing feedback arrows against an imaginary target without a bullseye.

One punishing economic aspect of a nomad team is its staying power; the ability to drone on endlessly with a project bolstered only by the prolific paperwork it spews as it moves along.

The meeting minutes cover desktops much as barnacles clinging to a pier. Volume belies the lack of accomplishment and substance. Months may tick by without useful results sufficient to fill a thimble.

Team members attend meetings not out of gusto or contributing results, but more likely to avoid reprimand for failed attendance. Bellwether signals exist to identify teams operating in this mode. They are:

1. Team life seems to be open ended with no concluding time frame in sight.
2. Minutes are rich in detail and widely distributed. But, is anybody reading them?
3. Team objectives not well defined or ambiguous.
4. Team has no idea what success will look like or when it has arrived.

**Back to square 1!**

## Nomad Teams
Wander aimlessly not certain where they are going or when they will arrive.

## Powerless Teams

Powerless teams may be innocent victims who can do everything right in project management except influence the implementation of their findings. They are sterile for all practical purposes.

Every element of their operation may have been well executed but when it comes to effect the changes, they are powerless. One aspect of a powerless team is the absence of a budget to fund the resources needed or conscript help.

Power comes in different forms, such as:

- Legitimate  -  Rank or title within an organization
- Intellectual  -  Knowledge in a given area
- Skills  -  Capability in applying knowledge
- Influence  -  Interpersonal or physical attraction
- Incentive  -  Ability to reward or compensate
- No power  -  Ability to extract fairness

It is most important when structuring a team to include members who command respect in the various forms of power.

## Slave Teams

Slave teams are in a no win situation by design. In the extreme, they exist to run cover for an unpopular decision yet to be announced. Team members are guided by their sponsors through a maze which ultimately leads to a preconceived outcome.

A slave team is not unusual in the conduct of a Job Assessment Center. A Job Assessment Center, as expressed here, is a method to evaluate the relative merits of multiple candidates vying for a job opening. Evaluators are chosen to rate the candidates as they perform different exercises and end with a consensus. Ratings are confidential to the group and the outcome is not binding on the decision maker. In this way, the decision maker can more readily escape the piercing wrath of an internal candidate who might not be chosen. And, in fact, a fait acompli on the choice may have occurred prior to the assessment process.

Another tactic employed is to add an external consultant to the slave team presumably as an objective, disinterested Ad Hoc member. The consultant performs interviews, takes surveys, interprets findings, and provides documentation which comes as no surprise supporting the beliefs of the echelon paying the bills.

## Mechanical Teams

Aside from fried onions, nothing leaves more acrid aftertaste than the workings of the phenomenon I call the mechanical team.

The most singular attribute of a mechanical team is its nearly total absence of warmth. The team is dead, at least in spirit, but doesn't know it or acknowledge it publicly. Regimentation rules supreme and power faces are the rule of the day. Formal rules are in place dictating an apparent business-like process that will govern the team's proceedings. Emphasis is more on form than function. The I's will be dotted, the T's crossed, and detailed minutes published on time.

The sad part of this scenario is that to a non-astute observer, the group dynamics would seem so correct. No nonsense here. Neat and tidy. Giving the devil his due, on the plus side, the process is predictable and orderly. On the negative side, the workings are contrived, boring, redundant, and uninspiring. Creativity is lacking. Serendipity is lacking. There is little or no fun during team member interaction.

Actions of the chairperson are the most obvious tip-off that a mechanical team exists. If he/she calls most of the shots and displays a Theory X autocratic management style, chances are the team will function in a mechanical style. Another hint is the seating arrangement at the formal meetings. If the chair commands the end position alone (carving the turkey) or arranges the chairs in a fan arrangement, then look out. A mechanical mode of operation is nearly certain.

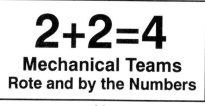

**2+2=4**
**Mechanical Teams**
**Rote and by the Numbers**

# Plastic Team

A plastic team, as the term suggests, is somewhat artificial with members acting in roles dissimilar to their normal mode of operation. It's an Alphonse-Gaston act. Fortunately, the plastic team phenomenon is not a lasting one. It usually occurs following a visit by an external consultant or expert in interpersonal relations. Coaching is done on the need for very formal, rigid rules governing the conduct of individuals as they go through the group dynamic process. It involves pledges of contractual trust. And, even though one was a rascal all his life, hereafter he would emulate Simon Pure while on the team. Initially, in its most formal sense, members would be asked to write formal contracts with each other - much in the same context of a legal document.

The problem with much of this process is that the members will be worrying more about form than function and more about detail than the objective warranted by the project.

Team members dance around each others sensitivities doing a lateral arabesque.

What is really needed goes far beyond a piece of paper with double signatures.

## MUTUALLY ALIGNED COMMITMENT

While team members may fully comprehend the stated objective, one or more members may withhold services. While this attitude and performance is not laudatory, there could be circumstances that invite this particular response.

Some of the more prominent ones are highlighted here along with some suggested antidotes to correct the failings.

## Project Deemed Unimportant or Boring

There are such things as Mickey Mouse Projects or time-worn efforts that seem to have an immortal, if not illustrious life. No one wants to participate on them, particularly those individuals with *can do* attitudes.

Recognition for Participation on this Team not Forthcoming

Perhaps you have been diligently working on this difficult project for some time, yet no one seems to notice or care. While you do not have a giant ego, you begin to think that it is a project whose outcome will not be valued in the least. No feedback has been heard regarding meeting minutes, and you wonder if they are even read.

## Team Member's Supervisor Displays Low Level of Interest

Supervisor did not initiate the team effort and now rarely shows even a modicum of interest in the progress. It is apparent that little added respect will be gained from participation in the team project. In fact, a sarcastic remark on the futility or shallowness of the project might be a cue to expend your energies elsewhere.

## Individuals Overwhelmed by Priorities Elsewhere

Even though well intentioned, an individual team member might have to pick and choose which meeting to attend: much like a debt-ridden person sorting out which bills to pay and which to defer for a time.

## Project Anticipated Outcome Inconsistent with an Individual's Personal Values

Results wanted by team or project sponsors does not hold well with an individual's personal values

## Unpopular Outcome

The eventual outcome might be unpopular and hazardous to one's work career. Territorial fiefdom's and political issues play havoc with the team's processes and discourage continued effort.

| COUNTERMEASURES FOR DEALING WITH MIS-ALIGNED TEAM COMMITMENT | |
|---|---|
| **SYMPTOMS** | POSSIBLE SOLUTIONS |
| 1. Project Deemed Unimportant | Better match of participants and task. |
| 2. Recognition Lacking | Celebrate wins, use good management practice. |
| 3. Supervisor's Disinterest | Supervisor initiative. Discuss with team member in one on one meetings, and staff get togethers. |
| 4. Individual Overburdened | Reassign individual, shed some tasks, or engage in a pep talk. |
| 5. Objective Inconsistent with Individuals personal value | This one hard to detect and hard to cure. Re-examine project scope for validity. |
| 6. Outcome Hazardous to individual participants | Backing and support from the proper management levels. |

# SINGLE SOLUTION FIXATION

Single solution fixations occurs more often with individuals within a team than the team as a whole. And, of course, it is human nature to particularly like one's own idea. It is a condition wherein a team member, or members, becomes grossly enamored with a particular idea or solution to a problem: usually early in the process. So much so, they hit an imaginary wall where they not only stop searching for other solutions, but they gloss over other ideas on the table also. Divergent thinking has quickly taken a back seat to convergent thinking.

In team efforts, the problem or objective being considered is a complex one; otherwise, a team would not be necessary to confront the problem. Consequently, solutions to demanding problems are not as obvious as apples on a tree waiting to be picked. Much thought and creative juices must flow in order to come up with an optimum or worthy solution. Except in rare cases, there exists not just a single solution to an opportunity, but rather an array of possibilities. Idea evaluations must consider both near and long term consequences, risks, resources available, and the degree of perfection required.

Single solution fixations are common in team efforts and present an interesting challenge. Several how to's face the team leader in particular. How to reopen the floor for further idea generation. How to solicit additional ideas without offending those holding a Single Solution Fixation. How to insure that all ideas that were generated, including the enamored idea, will get a fair hearing.

Several tactful and strategic techniques are available not only to help prevent the Single Solution Fixation, but to get them to be open minded again, as well. They are:

- Upfront, in the idea generation process, borrow two principles from Alex Osborn's Brainstorming Rules: go for a specific number of ideas and defer judgment during this phase.

- Emphasize vertical or divergent thinking: delay lateral or convergent thinking.

- Time pressures breed Single Solution Fixation. If the objective is worthy enough, then conventional wisdom suggests the team should be allotted sufficient time to work at the right tempo.

- Invoke the Idea Advocate technique to insure that all ideas get a fair hearing.

The Idea Advocate technique, used by Battelle Institute of Frankfort, features the team leader assigning various ideas to individual team members. Their role is to act as an advocate for the assigned ideas, expressing the idea's virtues to the listening members. It matters not who suggested the idea originally.

# CHAPTER ELEVEN
## TEAM SURVEYS AND FEEDBACK

I must express some ambivalence in the use of surveys to enhance team effectiveness by ultimately seeking to modify team behavior. Wrongly handled, the process may well achieve the opposite effect – less cohesiveness and trust than might have existed prior to the survey.

At the very least, a caution flag should be hoisted when undertaking peer evaluations of team members' performance. Let me illustrate.

I recall one team building session where a large group of employees in a classroom setting were being guided by an external consultant. She circulated a survey in which we were asked to anonymously evaluate each person on a series of sensitive points. The feedback was to be tabulated, totaled, and hung on the wall for all to see. The thought was that, in frankness, all could publicly see the scores, and ultimately address areas of weakness.

Included in the group was the executive staff who, indecently, did not fare badly in this process. It may have had something to do with a subordinate's fear of having his handwriting recognized.

You might anticipate the disaster which occurred. Sheltering their fear of being low in relative ranking, in front of superiors, many of the charmed group rated all others as low as possible. Others, it appeared, mistook the number one to be a high rating, (1-10), while it actually represented the lowest possible rating.

The result was an abbreviated team building session, hard feelings among the members, and, believe it or not, the well-meaning consultant in tears.

And yet, in another Work Improvement Seminar I attended, the instructor advocated a similar concept for building teams.

The instructor had just completed a lengthy discourse on the need for absolute trust, candor, and openness among team members, then followed it up with feedback survey examples that omitted the names of those providing critical feedback to a team member. Openness and trust? I'm thinking that an individual receiving some severe criticism from an anonymous source might spend a lot of time fretting over which trusted team member broadsided him in print, but was reluctant to do it faceside.

As a routine means of evaluating team interaction, surveys might well be a waste of time. What is really important is whether or not the task is being achieved within the parameters established. Is progress being made? Surveys have their place in the process of evaluating employee attitudes in the work place. Normally, these fare better when used in a broader context and designed and interpreted by those professionals knowing what they are doing. A facsimile of one style survey is illustrated for your review.

---

### TEAM SELF ASSESSMENT SURVEY
### ILLUSTRATED IN BRIEF:
### TWO TYPES:  QUALITATIVE AND QUANTITATIVE

| QUALITATIVE | QUANTITATIVE |
|---|---|
| **OBJECTIVES** | **OBJECTIVES** |
| \_\_\_\_\_a.  Team Objective is fuzzy or inconsequential. | Objective is fuzzy —— Objective clear and acceptable |
| \_\_\_\_\_b.  Team has lost focus. | ⌊\_\|\_\_\|\_\_\|\_\_\| x \| (x at 5) |
| \_X\_c.  Objective is clear and mutually acceptable. | 1    2    3    4    5 |
| **COMMITMENT** | **COMMITMENT** |
| \_X\_a.  Noticeably low level of team commitment. | Low Level Commitment —— Noticeably Committed |
| \_\_\_\_\_b.  Team members exhibit reasonable commitment through attendance and performance. | ⌊\_\| x \|\_\_\|\_\_\| \| (x at 2) |
| \_\_\_\_\_c.  Team is highly committed and participates effectively. | 1    2    3    4    5 |
| **COMMUNICATIONS** | **COMMUNICATIONS** |
| \_\_\_\_\_a.  Closed and ineffective. | Closed and ineffective —— Candid, cordial and effective |
| \_X\_b.  Mixed communications. Sometimes lacking in harmony. | ⌊\_\|\_\_\| x \|\_\_\| \| (x at 3) |
| \_\_\_\_\_c.  Open, candid communications are effective and cordial. | 1    2    3    4    5 |

# Feedback

Much has been written about the necessity and manner in which to provide feedback. While having some thoughts on the subject, master I'm not. However, I will provide some criteria that has worked well for me over the years, particularly in team settings. Having a wife and three daughters has honed my feedback skills to the point that, like Ross Perot, I measure three times – cut once.

1. Unfavorable feedback should be as rare as the sightings of the American Bald Eagle. And, feedback about which a team member can do nothing about should be as rare as a Dodo bird.

2. Unfavorable feedback generally occurs out of the critical parent ego state. Try to curve the feedback to the positive side, coming out of the nurturing parent ego state.

3. Critical feedback to a team member should be delivered in private, in an informal setting.

4. Timing and specificity of the feedback given are important issues.

5. When attempting feedback, omit starting out with the phrase, "I'm going to give you some constructive criticism." Believe me, the receiver will not find the news as constructive as the sender, and the forewarning is equal to the patient awaiting a proctoscopic examination.

6. Focus your feedback on the issue of results rather than personal behavior.

7. Solicited feedback is easier to swallow than unwelcome, surprise broadsides.

8. If you, as a team leader, don't provide positive feedback, then feel free to omit negative feedback as well.

---

## A DOZEN AND ONE REASONS TEAMS FAIL

1. Not a valid project to begin with.

2. Never clear what the objective really was.

3. Outcome would be hazardous to someone's health - their own perhaps.

4. Project died under it's own weight - took too long to develop.

5. Team members left, transferred or reassigned other priorities.

6. Capability of team leader lacking.

7. Inadequate resources or funding.

8. Inexperienced team members who knew not what to do.

9. Team worried about show than flow; form than function.

10. Team members were incompatible.

11. Team was unenthused about the task.

12. Superiors demonstrated little or no interest in project reports.

13. Team members were just plain lazy.

## CHARACTERISTICS OF TEAMS

| EFFECTIVE TEAMS | INEFFECTIVE TEAMS |
|---|---|
| **A. Upfront Planning**<br><br>Members pleased with the assignment | Members see it as another chore |
| Appropriate skills and knowledge reside in team members | Warm bodies being key requirement or availability |
| Objective is clear | Hazy, ill defined objective |
| Valid undertaking to noticeability of all | Questionable undertaking |
| **B. Meeting Dynamics**<br><br>Face to face meetings or ingenuous advanced electronic devices. | Meetings are catch as catch can, often by phone hookups or Fax machine |
| Regular meetings at adequate intervals | Irregular scheduling and frequency of meetings either too much or too little |
| Meetings have an egalitarian ring | Meetings autocratic or dominated by a few |
| Organized agenda and follow through | Helter skelter come what may immersion into topics |
| Candid, open differences expressed and accepted | Hostile at one end of the spectrum, groupthink at the other |
| Mutual trust and respect | Hidden agendas |

# CHAPTER TWELVE
## MEETINGS: GOOD & BAD

### PRODUCTIVE MEETINGS

Meetings having ten or more participants can be a challenge to manage properly. Meetings of this magnitude generally serve purposes of gathering/providing information or identifying issues. On this score, they do all right. But, large group meetings seldom provide the right forum for effective problem solving, particularly if the problems are complex ones.

What is often noticeable in large gatherings is the wasteful efficiency loss. When one participant speaks, the others are compelled to listen. The attention span of participants is usually proportional to the length of the session, vitality of the subject, and closeness to mealtime.

Another phenomenon in big meetings is the difficulty in being heard, even if one has something valuable to say on the subject. It is not unusual for at least two or three loquacious members in a group this large to dominate floor time vocalizing their "pearls of wisdom".

Large meetings should generally be avoided unless they are for the shear purpose of sharing information or identifying issues.

You can increase the prospects of having a productive first meeting, setting the stage for subsequent success, by following seven prerequisites, being:

1. Think it through – "Is a meeting really necessary?"

2. Determine topic and scope.

3. Select the right participants.

4. Determine logistics.
   Initial meeting:
   > Date, Time, Location, Duration

5. Select a room well suited for the meeting.

6. Inquire in advance of a participant's availability to attend.

7. Send written invitations, including agenda.

## COMPARATIVE ADVANTAGES AND SHORTCOMINGS OF BIG VS SMALLER GROUP MEETINGS

| MEETING ATTRIBUTES | BIG GROUPS (EXCESS OF 20 PARTICIPANTS) | SMALLER GROUPS (DOZEN OR FEWER PARTICIPANTS |
|---|---|---|
| **I. Informational** | | |
| One-way communication | **Effective** | **Neutral** |
| Announcements/policy changes | **Effective** | **Neutral** |
| Number of meeting needed | **Fewer to cover large number** | **More meetings and more time needed** |
| Message interpretation | **All hear the same message** | **Chance for inconsistency** |
| Two way dialogue | **Very difficult** | **Inviting** |
| **II. Effectiveness** | | |
| Process Losses | **Very high** | **Effective possibilities** |
| Productivity | **Unlikely** | **Enhanced** |
| Problem Solving | **Difficult** | **Enhanced** |
| Decision Making | **Difficult** | **Enhanced** |
| Redundancy | **Likely** | **Managed** |
| **III. Environmental** | | |
| Available meeting sites | **Limited** | **Enhanced** |
| Comfort | **Inflexible** | **Flexible** |
| **IV. Focus and Control** | **At risk** | **Reasonably manageable** |

## DOWNSIDE OF COMMITTEES AND MEETINGS

There has been a plethora of less than favorable comments about committees and meetings. While some comments are no doubt made in casual jest; on the whole, a lot of fruitless meetings have occurred. Otherwise, we would not experience the unending flow of disparaging testimony. Following is just a few famous quotations on the subject of meetings and committees.

## TEAM MEETING DYNAMICS

| ENHANCEMENTS | DETRACTORS |
| --- | --- |
| One hour meetings | Routine meetings exceeding two hours |
| Agenda | Winging it |
| Review open action items | Glossing over inactivity |
| Composed discussion | Fiery rhetoric |
| Voiced concerns | Lamb like group think |
| Some dutiful listening | Rambling prattle |
| Morning meetings, except Monday | Mid afternoon meetings |
| Open candor | Manipulation |
| Listening exceeds talking | Loquacious |

## INSTITUTIONAL MEETINGS

It has been my experience that institutional meetings, such as those of school boards and city councils, do not run as smoothly as that of business counterparts. After thinking about it, this revelation should come as no surprise.

The difference is precisely in the nature of the team with it's cohesiveness; and that of a group of individuals loosely constructed. Brought together by the election process, councils and boards do not ordinarily share a common workplace, trained together, or necessarily have common interests or reasons for running for office.

Business teams ordinarily do; it is likely that team members have worked together on a variety of prior projects, not always the same mix. Beyond this, candidates for school boards are motivated to run for the non-paying positions (in most states) for reasons that range all the way from altruism to hidden agendas.

After watching the subject meetings in action, a paradox occurs to me. While board and council meetings are more formal in a sense, using Roberts Rules of Order, etc., and business team meetings do not, business team meetings seem much more robust in the use of visual aids, supporting data, systematic techniques, and logic in their proceedings. This is due to internal training programs and relationships that may exceed decades.

Let me illustrate two examples of institution meetings I attended as a guest and impressions that followed.

## City Council Meeting:

Council met to hear proposals by an out of state developer who wanted to construct low income townhousing in the community. These units would largely be subsidized by the federal government, with a high turnover of residents a distinct possibility.

The developer proposed acquiring city owned land of pristine woodlands, nearly gratis, and building thereon.

This proposal made little sense to the neighbors adjacent to the proposed site, whose home values and taxes were among the highest in the city, and they felt threatened. That's the scenario.

Seated on council were seven voting members. For this multi-million dollar development, the developer made his articulate pitch without so much as a single exhibit or notes on the back of a matchbook. He was smooth and polished, but not necessarily forthcoming to questions addressed of him.

The developer further insisted that he needed a decision that very night; right then. The council seemed moved to action. I wondered why. Those pristine mountains had been there since the glacial drift, maybe the PRE-Paleozoic period, and acting hastily seemed a contrived thought devoid of substance.

Arguments from the floor were heated with good points being made during a two hour period.

It was nearly a foregone conclusion that the developer would eventually gain approval. One council member was reportedly heard to say after the meeting conclusion – "better on your hill than mine." This was heresay.

In the end, the project was approved with modifications increasing the distance between the existing and proposed low income housing.

The council meeting could have been greatly enhanced had a "team: atmosphere, among council, the developer and the neighbors been followed. The ingredients that weren't present that would have added much were:

- Objective appraisal of the value to the community.
- Visual aids during the developer's proposal.

- A flipchart highlighting neighbor's concerns.
- Use of problem solving techniques to address those concerns, such as force field analysis.
- Other missing attributes were:
  - Mutual trust, respect and shared values.

This was no fun meeting.

## School Board Meeting

Due to late season enrollment increases, three first grade classes in a community were faced with upwards of thirty students; an appalling number for appropriate early childhood learning. Action to alleviate this condition through class size reductions, was not forthcoming, therefore concerned parents went to the initial school board meeting to cite their concerns.

The first board meeting didn't materialize as there was no quorum. Try as the attending members might in phone calls, a fifth member did not show. Approximately eighty frustrated friends of education and parents spent two hours, essentially wasting 160 man/woman hours, to no avail.

The second meeting subsequently scheduled, proved no better than the first in convincing the board to reduce class size; a 5-4 vote against restructuring class size. This dialogue is not intended to weight the merits of the case, but rather to point out what appeared to be deficiencies in the meeting process – moving it farther away from tenets of the team process.

Deficiencies were:

1. Aside from being on the formal agenda, all citizens with comments from the floor had to be identified up front.

2. All registered speakers from the audience were given the podium to present their message first; and did, without comment or dialogue from the board.

3. Input from the floor ended at that point. No further debate of challenge was allowed except among board members. Audience became spectators who then could only react through clapping, hissing or booing.

4. If a board member expressed a concept of dubious accuracy or sound thought, it became a moot point as counterviews were not aired.

5. There was an absence of mutual trust, respect and dialogue.

This meeting and outcome reinforces the natural differences between a team concept, and a group or cluster gathered together to conduct business.

## ILLUSTRATED GOOD TEAM MEETING; IDEA REVIEW TEAM

SCENARIO:    All four members are present and on time at a regularly scheduled team meeting, sitting at a round table. Previous meeting minutes are in hands. Greetings have been made.

Meeting room has flipcharts and other visual aid equipment that may or may not be necessary.

Leader - "This will be a brief but important meeting today. Our annual recognition dinner is coming up shortly and we want to have as many of the people who submitted ideas, eligible for the dinner as possible. Let's go over the open ideas. Mary, you have two open ones. Any progress?

Mary – "Yes, Idea F-106 by Andrea Loudermilk is now implemented and the annual savings is projected to be $450,000."

Leader - "Good work! That will please Andrea as she is now eligible for the dinner. She's been anxious about it and just yesterday inquired on the status. What about Mel Simpson's idea concerning using halogen lights?"

Mary - "That one we had to deep six. I discussed the idea with him, going over the numbers and reasons it won't be feasible at the time. He is satisfied and sees the rationale. He isn't discouraged and has another idea or two up his sleeve."

Leader - "Thanks Mary. Let's see, Homer - you didn't have any new ideas open to review for this meeting; you're off the hook. Co-Co, you had one still open; any news?"

Co-Co Guy - "I'm still checking Bill Bennet's idea on using a casting instead of a weldment on the main frame. The foundry is expected to provide their quotation by next Monday. Also, while I was at it, I sent a drawing to Cyclops Company to see what they might quote to make the finished part complete. That's all I had."

Leader - "OK, that takes care of the open ideas. We only have one new idea today. I'll distribute a copy to each of you, then after you read it, we will discuss it's merits."

Leader - "Hmmmm, Jolene thinks that the internal maintenance staff can paint the training room less expensively than the contract painters who have been doing our other work. What do you think?"

Homer - "I think Jolene has something there worth investigating. The contractor's prices have risen dramatically in the past year. I'll query the contractors and get their firm bid for the job."

Mary - "It is probably that internally we now have the resources available. I'll get a cost figure and when their schedule might permit. It would be good from a control standpoint to keep the work inside."

Leader - "Sounds good. Let's do it. Co-Co Guy - anything to add?"

Co-Co Guy - "Yes, do we have to have that ugly pink color again? Give it a rest!"

Leader - "Forget it Co-Co. Old Bosso thinks it has a calming influence. OK. Thanks team for your efforts. We'll meet again two weeks from today. I'll put out the meeting minutes. Again, remember that the deadline for the recognition dinner is nearing. Meeting adjourned."

The preceding was a microcosm of an effective team meeting and was intentionally kept brief for illustration purposes. However, the illustration is factually close to the manner in which effective idea review teams do operate.

---

### IMPACT MEETINGS - T.R. KING

- Stands the test of really being the pragmatic way to address a particular situation

- An agenda exists and, at the very least, a glint of the outcome anticipated

- Those team members urgent to the process are present

- Highly detailed work is not plowed though at the meeting

- Continuity is preserved by reviewing action points and making new assignments

- Meeting lasts two hours or less for ordinary situations.

---

# QUOTATIONS

CHAPTER ONE                Alexander Graham Bell

CHAPTER TWO                H.E. Luccock

CHAPTER THREE              Vince Pfaff
                          Charles Kettering

CHAPTER FOUR               J. Ogden Armour
                          Knute Rockne
                          Bum Phillips
                          Thomas Carlyle

CHAPTER FIVE               Peter Ueberroth
                          Ross Perot
                          Douglas McGregor
                          Louis Pasteur

CHAPTER TWELVE             John K. Galbraith
                          Sir Barnett Cocks
                          J.B. Hughes
                          George David Keefer
                          Joe Taylor Ford

# REFERENCES

CHAPTER TWO            1.  Chris Wright, Franklin News Herald

CHAPTER THREE          2.  Ringelmann, German Psychologist

CHAPTER FOUR           3.  A. Chickering, Fork of Competency Concept

CHAPTER FIVE           4.  Alex Osborne, Brainstorming Techniques

                       5.  Council For Continuous Improvement,
                           Q.R. Resources

CHAPTER SIX            6.  Eric Berne, Transactional Analysis

CHAPTER SEVEN         7.  Joseph Luft & Harry Ingram,
                           JOHARI WINDOW Concept

                       8.  Arthur E. Mudge

CHAPTER EIGHT          9.  Dr. I.L. Janus, GROUPTHINK

CHAPTER NINE          10.  Dr. R.A. Fraser, SAVE PROCEEDINGS

# INDEX

# INDEX, CONTINUED

# ABOUT THE AUTHOR
## Thomas R. King, CVS, FSAVE

Tom King was raised on a small farm in Pennsylvania overlooking the Monongahela River. Two of his claims to fame are a baseball tryout with the Pittsburgh Pirates and being a world record holder in hoeing corn, the latter being unverified.

His hometown of Fredericktown was a coal-mining town rife with European immigrants, working-class people struggling to better their situation. Honest, decent, hardworking people who showed tolerance to all and malice toward none.

His father was uncontested as the only farmer in the community. Tom's mother, a teacher, instilled values early and often counseled, "Never take the petals from someone else's rose".

Tom's advice to all young men who would seek an extraordinarily happy life is to marry a coal miner's daughter. He did, Esther Heckler, and is indeed a happy man. Esther and Tom have three daughters, Andrea, Marcia and Krista.

Tom King is a Certified Value Specialist (CVS), a Past President of the Society of American Value Engineers, (SAVE) and an elected SAVE Fellow (FSAVE). He is a longtime member of the Society of Manufacturing Engineers (SME) and MENSA. Vocationally, he is the Division Manager of Value Engineering for Joy Mining Machinery, Harnischfeger Industries, Inc., based in Franklin, Pennsylvania. His company received the first corporate "Excellence in Value Engineering" award from SAVE.

He is a graduate of Pitt University and the University of the State of New York. He was a staff member at Pitt University teaching Value Engineering. He has authored books, articles and columns for many of the nation's leading industrial magazines, conducted workshops, and lectured extensively in academia and professional societies.

Thomas R. King is regarded internationally as a leading expert in the Value Engineering field.

# A FINAL THOUGHT

I have often wondered why some authors dedicate their works to a plethora of people ranging from loved ones to the school crossing guard and the oboe player in the second symphony row, it always seemed a bit much to me.

Now I know.

It comes with the realization that in no small way, an author owes much of his or her success, however modest, to others

I too owe thanks to many.

Esther – I dedicate this book to you.

Love,
The Fox